Wi-Fi Hotspots

Cisco Press

800 East 96th Street
Indianapolis, Indiana 46240 USA

Eric Geier

Wi-Fi Hotspots

Eric Geier

Copyright© 2007 Cisco Systems, Inc.

Published by:
Cisco Press
800 East 96th Street
Indianapolis, IN 46240 USA

Printed in the United States of America 1 2 3 4 5 6 7 8 9 0

First Printing: October 2006

Library of Congress Cataloging-in-Publication Number: 2006924238

ISBN: 1-58705-266-0

Warning and Disclaimer

This book is designed to provide information about installing, operating, and supporting Wi-Fi hotspots. Every effort has been made to make this book as complete and as accurate as possible, but no warranty or fitness is implied.

The information is provided on an "as is" basis. The author, Cisco Press, and Cisco Systems, Inc. shall have neither liability nor responsibility to any person or entity with respect to any loss or damages arising from the information contained in this book or from the use of the discs or programs that may accompany it.

The opinions expressed in this book belong to the author and are not necessarily those of Cisco Systems, Inc.

Trademark Acknowledgments

All terms mentioned in this book that are known to be trademarks or service marks have been appropriately capitalized. Cisco Press or Cisco Systems, Inc. cannot attest to the accuracy of this information. Use of a term in this book should not be regarded as affecting the validity of any trademark or service mark.

Publisher
Paul Boger

Cisco Representative
Anthony Wolfenden

Cisco Press Program Manager
Jeff Brady

Executive Editor
Brett Bartow

Managing Editor
Patrick Kanouse

Senior Development Editor
Christopher A. Cleveland

Senior Project Editor
San Dee Phillips

Copy Editor
Karen A. Gill

Technical Editors
Fred Niehaus
Jack Unger

Editorial Assistant
Vanessa Evans

Book and Cover Designer
Louisa Adair

Composition
Mark Shirar

Indexer
Tim Wright

Corporate and Government Sales

Cisco Press offers excellent discounts on this book when ordered in quantity for bulk purchases or special sales.

For more information please contact: U.S. Corporate and Government Sales **1-800-382-3419** **corpsales@pearsontechgroup.com**

For sales outside the U.S. please contact: International Sales **international@pearsoned.com**

Feedback Information

At Cisco Press, our goal is to create in-depth technical books of the highest quality and value. Each book is crafted with care and precision, undergoing rigorous development that involves the unique expertise of members from the professional technical community.

Readers' feedback is a natural continuation of this process. If you have any comments regarding how we could improve the quality of this book, or otherwise alter it to better suit your needs, you can contact us through e-mail at feedback@ciscopress.com. Please be sure to include the book title and ISBN in your message.

We greatly appreciate your assistance.

CISCO SYSTEMS

Corporate Headquarters
Cisco Systems, Inc.
170 West Tasman Drive
San Jose, CA 95134-1706
USA
www.cisco.com
Tel: 408 526-4000
     800 553-NETS (6387)
Fax: 408 526-4100

European Headquarters
Cisco Systems International BV
Haarlerbergpark
Haarlerbergweg 13-19
1101 CH Amsterdam
The Netherlands
www-europe.cisco.com
Tel: 31 0 20 357 1000
Fax: 31 0 20 357 1100

Americas Headquarters
Cisco Systems, Inc.
170 West Tasman Drive
San Jose, CA 95134-1706
USA
www.cisco.com
Tel: 408 526-7660
Fax: 408 527-0883

Asia Pacific Headquarters
Cisco Systems, Inc.
Capital Tower
168 Robinson Road
#22-01 to #29-01
Singapore 068912
www.cisco.com
Tel: +65 6317 7777
Fax: +65 6317 7799

Cisco Systems has more than 200 offices in the following countries and regions. Addresses, phone numbers, and fax numbers are listed on the **Cisco.com Web site at www.cisco.com/go/offices.**

Argentina • Australia • Austria • Belgium • Brazil • Bulgaria • Canada • Chile • China PRC • Colombia • Costa Rica • Croatia • Czech Republic Denmark • Dubai, UAE • Finland • France • Germany • Greece • Hong Kong SAR • Hungary • India • Indonesia • Ireland • Israel • Italy Japan • Korea • Luxembourg • Malaysia • Mexico • The Netherlands • New Zealand • Norway • Peru • Philippines • Poland • Portugal Puerto Rico • Romania • Russia • Saudi Arabia • Scotland • Singapore • Slovakia • Slovenia • South Africa • Spain • Sweden Switzerland • Taiwan • Thailand • Turkey • Ukraine • United Kingdom • United States • Venezuela • Vietnam • Zimbabwe

About the Author

Eric Geier is a computing and wireless networking author and consultant. For several years, he has been employed with Wireless-Nets, Ltd., a consulting firm focusing on the implementation of wireless mobile solutions and training.

Eric is a certified wireless network administrator (CWNA). He is an author of and contributor to several books and eLearning (CBT) courses. He is a regular contributor at Wi-FiPlanet.com.

For more information about Eric, visit his website at http://www.egeier.com.

Companion Website

The following website was created by the author, Eric Geier, to promote the book:

http://www.wifihotspotbook.com <http://www.wifihotspotbook.com/

Readers of this book can access a special section of the website which contains convenient links and useful information about the products and topics brought up in the book:

http://www.wifihotspotbook.com/bonus_materials/

About the Technical Reviewers

Fred Niehaus is a technical marketing engineer for the Wireless Networking Business Unit at Cisco Systems, Inc. Fred has extensive customer contact and is responsible for developing and marketing enterprise-class wireless solutions using Cisco Aironet and Airespace series wireless LAN products.

Fred has actively participated in some of the largest Cisco wireless LAN deployments in education and retail, with such customers as the New York Board of Education and the Home Depot stores.

Before joining the Cisco wireless networking business unit, via the acquisition of Aironet, Fred worked as a support engineer for Telxon Inc., supporting some of the first wireless implementations from customers such as WalMart, Ford, Hertz Rent-A-Car, and others.

Jack Unger founded Wireless InfoNet (now Ask-Wi.Com, Inc.) in 1993, a turnkey outdoor broadband wireless WAN solutions provider. Since 1993, Jack has served more than 1000 client companies, providing network design, installation, optimization, support, training, consulting, and technical writing for the wireless networking industry. In 1995, he deployed one of the first wireless ISPs in the world, operating on 900 MHz in Los Altos Hills, California.

Since 2001, in workshops across the United States and Canada, Jack has trained more than 2000 ISP personnel to design, deploy, and support outdoor wireless networks. He wrote the vendor-neutral industry handbook *Deploying License-Free Wireless Wide-Area Networks*, which was published by Cisco Press in 2003.

Before founding Wireless InfoNet, Jack spent 14 years working in the Silicon Valley telecommunications industry with ROLM, IBM, Siemens, and NEC. At ROLM, Jack led the QA Systems Audit Group. At IBM and Siemens, as a senior associate technical writer, he authored more than 100 PBX hardware and software technical manuals. At NEC, he served as a telecommunications analyst for the NEC global networking group. Before his telecommunications industry career, Jack worked for seven years in San Jose and Scotts Valley, California, selling wireless communications equipment, including television and radio station broadcast equipment.

Dedication

This book is dedicated to my beautiful wife, Sierra, and my goofy daughter, Madison. You two make all the hard work worth it!

Acknowledgments

I would like to give special recognition to Jim Geier for listening to my ideas and for the valuable tips and feedback that made this book even better.

Thanks to Scott Tully and Gary McKinney from Public IP for providing information about ZoneCD and for letting me include their hotspot software on the accompanying CD for this book.

I would also like to thank everyone at Cisco Press for making this book possible. It has been a pleasure working with such an outstanding publisher.

This Book Is Safari Enabled

The Safari® Enabled icon on the cover of your favorite technology book means the book is available through Safari Bookshelf. When you buy this book, you get free access to the online edition for 45 days.

Safari Bookshelf is an electronic reference library that lets you easily search thousands of technical books, find code samples, download chapters, and access technical information whenever and wherever you need it.

To gain 45-day Safari Enabled access to this book:

- Go to http://www.ciscopress.com/safarienabled

- Complete the brief registration form

- Enter the coupon code 1JKY-3GZJ-JGJ4-ZEJ3-KWG1

If you have difficulty registering on Safari Bookshelf or accessing the online edition, please e-mail customer-service@safaribooksonline.com.

Contents at a Glance

Part I: The Basics   3

Chapter 1   The Basics of Wi-Fi Hotspots   5

Chapter 2   The Business Side of Hosting a Hotspot   19

Chapter 3   First Steps to Setting Up a Wi-Fi Hotspot   33

Part II: Setting Up the Hotspot   49

Chapter 4   Solution 1: Simple Free Access Hotspot   51

Chapter 5   Solution 2: Advanced Free Access Hotspot Using ZoneCD   65

Chapter 6   Solution 3: Join Boingo's Hotspot Network to Provide Paid Access   107

Chapter 7   Solution 4: Free or Paid Access and Private Network Using Hotspot Gateway   117

Part III: After Your Wi-Fi Hotspot Is Alive   133

Chapter 8   Getting the Word Out   135

Chapter 9   Fending Off Freeloaders   143

Chapter 10   Wi-Fi Safety and Security   151

Chapter 11   Common Problems and Fixes   163

Chapter 12   Increasing Your Hotspot's Wireless Coverage   171

Chapter 13   Using Wi-Fi Networks   197

Part IV: Appendix   219

Appendix A   Understanding Wi-Fi Signals   221

Glossary   237

Index   240

Contents

Part I: The Basics 3

Chapter 1   The Basics of Wi-Fi Hotspots   5
              Bridging the Gap   7
              Wi-Fi Hot Zones   10
              How Users Find Hotspots   12
              How Wi-Fi Works   14
              Chapter Review   16

Chapter 2   The Business Side of Hosting a Hotspot   19
              Benefits of Hosting a Wi-Fi Hotspot   19
                  Attract People to Your Location   19
                  Generate Additional Revenue   20
                      Increased Sales of Products or Services   21
                      Hotspot Network Commissions   22
                      Fees from an Independent Fee-Based Hotspot   23
                      Advertising Revenue   25
                  Ability to Create a Private Network   26
              Figuring the Costs   29
              Chapter Review   31

Chapter 3   First Steps to Setting Up a Wi-Fi Hotspot   33
              Step 1: Choose a Hotspot Solution   33
                  Solution 1: Simple Free Access Hotspot   34
                  Solution 2: Advanced Free Access Hotspot Using ZoneCD   34
                  Solution 3: Boingo's Hotspot Network to Provide Paid Access   34
                  Solution 4: Free or Paid Access and Private Network Using a Hotspot
                    Gateway   34
                  Hotspot Features   35
                  Additional Solutions   38
              Step 2: Set Up an Internet Connection   40
                  Choosing the Right Internet Connect Type   40
                      "Always-On" Internet Connections   41
                      DSL Internet Connections   41
                      Fixed Wireless Broadband   42
                      Cable Internet Connections   42
                      T1 Internet Connections   42
                      Satellite   43
                      Questions to Ask ISPs   43
                  Usage/Legal Terms of Provider   45
                  Getting the Internet Connection   45
                      Where to Install the Connection   46
              Chapter Review   47

Part II: Setting Up the Hotspot   49

Chapter 4   Solution 1: Simple Free Access Hotspot   51
             Step 1: Gather the Necessary Items   52
             Step 2: Set Up the Wireless Router   52
             Step 3: Configure Additional Settings   53
                 Accessing the Web-Based Configuration Utility   53
                 DHCP User Limit   54
                 AP Isolation   55
                 VPN Passthrough   56
                 Access Restrictions   57
                 Blocked Services   58
                 Remote Router Access   59
                 Web-Based Configuration Utility Access Server   60
                 Backup Configuration   61
             Chapter Review   62

Chapter 5   Solution 2: Advanced Free Access Hotspot Using ZoneCD   65
             Step 1: Choose the Mode and Service   67
                 Open Mode   67
                 Closed Mode   68
                 Services Overview   70
                     Splash Screen   71
                     Content Filtering   72
                     User Classes   72
                     Bandwidth Throttling   73
                     Time and Transfer Limits   73
                     Open/Close Hours   73
                     Walled Garden   73
                     Firewall   74
                     Reports   74
                     Ticket System   74
                     Network Availability Hours   74
                     Spot Check   74
                     Hotspot Directory   75
                     Network Printer   75
                     Configuration Queue   75
                     Templates   75
                     Customize E-Mails   76
             Step 2: Gather the Necessary Items   76
                 What's Required   76
                     Private Wired or Wireless Router   77
                     Public Access Point or Wireless Router   78
                     Computer   80
                     The ZoneCD Disc   81

Set Up Your Zones (for the Free Service)   82
Set Up Your Zones (for the Premium Services)   83
Step 3: Set Up and Configure the Access Points and Routers   84
Private Wired or Wireless Router   84
Public Access Point or Wireless Router   85
Step 4: Perform a Physical Installation   88
Step 5: Perform ZoneCD Initial Setup   88
The Boot Process   89
Open Mode Configuration   97
Closed Mode (Free Server) Configuration   98
Closed Mode (Premium Server) Configuration   100
Check for Proper Operation   102
What's Next   103
Using the Online Administration Tools   103
Getting Help   103
Chapter Review   105

Chapter 6   Solution 3: Join Boingo's Hotspot Network to Provide Paid
                  Access   107
Understanding the Solution   107
Setting Up the Solution   107
Step 1: Gather the Necessary Items   108
Step 2: Set Up the Equipment   109
Step 3: Join Boingo's Hotspot Network   110
Step 4: Perform the Physical Installation   111
Placing the Wireless Router   111
Check for Proper Operation   114
Getting Help   114
Chapter Review   114

Chapter 7   Solution 4: Free or Paid Access and Private Network Using Hotspot
                  Gateway   117
Understanding the Solution   117
Setting Up the Solution   118
Step 1: Choose the Particular Solution   118
Free Access Options   118
Paid Access Options   119
Step 2: Gather the Necessary Items   120
Hotspot Gateway   120
Ticket Printer   121
RADIUS Server   122
Step 3: Set Up the Equipment   122
Hotspot Gateway Setup   122
Ticket Printer Setup   125
RADIUS Server Setup   126

Step 4: Configure Additional Settings   126
Step 5: Perform the Physical Installation   127
   Placing the Gateway   128
   Check for Proper Operation   130
Getting Help   130
Chapter Review   130

Part III: After Your Wi-Fi Hotspot Is Alive   133

Chapter 8   Getting the Word Out   135
Signage   135
Advertisements   137
Online Hotspot Directories   137
Chapter Review   141

Chapter 9   Fending Off Freeloaders   143
Physically Hand Out Login Information   143
Apply Usage Limits   143
   Open/Closed Times   143
   Bandwidth Limits   145
Spell Out Usage Terms   146
Monitor Your Hotspot   147
Chapter Review   149

Chapter 10   Wi-Fi Safety and Security   151
Understanding Everyone's Responsibilities   151
Hotspot Administrator/Owner Responsibilities   151
   Inform Users of the Risks   152
   Give Users Safety and Security Tips   154
   Enable VPN Passthrough   155
   Isolate Clients   155
   Filter Hotspot Content   156
   Secure User Information   158
User Responsibilities   158
   Beware of the Risks   158
   Follow the Safety and Security Tips   159
   Use VPN Connections   159
   Use Secure (SSL) Websites   159
   Disable File Sharing   160
   Use a Personal Firewall   160
   Keep an Eye on Valuables   160
Chapter Review   160

Chapter 11   Common Problems and Fixes   163
             Unable to See/Connect to the Wi-Fi Hotspot   163
                  What the User Should Do   163
                  What You Should Do   163
             Frequent Disconnections   164
                  What the User Should Do   164
                  What You Should Do   165
             Poor Performance   165
                  What the User Should Do   165
                  What You Should Do   165
             Internet Connection Unavailable   166
                  What the User Should Do   167
                  What You Should Do   167
             Where to Find More Help   168
             Chapter Review   169

Chapter 12   Increasing Your Hotspot's Wireless Coverage   171
             Higher-Gain Antenna   171
                  Purchasing   174
                  Installation   175
             Wireless Repeaters   175
                  Purchasing   177
                  Installation   178
             Adding Access Points   178
                  Preinstallation Site Survey   179
                       Step 1: Gather the Necessary Items   180
                       Step 2: Define the Network Requirements   181
                       Step 3: Mark Up the Building Diagram   182
                       Step 4: Determine the AP Locations   183
                  Network and Power Connection Options   189
                       Power Lines   190
                       Running Ethernet Cable   191
                  Choosing and Purchasing Your Equipment   192
                       Access Points   192
                       Power Line Devices   192
                       Ethernet Cable   193
                       PoE   193
                  Configuring the APs   194
                  Physical Installation   194
             Chapter Review   195

Chapter 13   Using Wi-Fi Networks   197

      Keeping Your Operating System Up-to-Date   197

      Enabling and Disabling Your Network Adapter   197

          Using the Start Menu   197

          Using the System Tray   198

      Toggling Between Windows XP and the Manufacturer Utility   199

          Enabling/Disabling the Windows XP Utility   199

          Starting/Stopping the Wireless Zero Configuration Service   201

      Connecting to a Wi-Fi Network Using the Windows XP Configuration Utility   202

      Checking the Connection Status   203

          Using the System Tray   203

          Using the Status Window   204

      Editing Your Preferred Network List   205

          Accessing the Preferred Network List   205

          Changing the Preferred Order   206

          Adding a Preferred Network   207

          Advanced Options   210

      Sharing Files   210

          Enabling Shared Folders   211

          Accessing Shared Folders   212

      Sharing Printers   214

          Enabling Shared Printers   214

          Adding Shared Printers to Computers   215

      Chapter Summary   217

Part IV: Appendix   219

Appendix A   Understanding Wi-Fi Signals   221

Glossary   237

Index   240

Introduction

Users of wireless networks at home and work can move about their office or home with their laptops and PDAs, checking e-mail, browsing the web, and swapping files between PCs. Wi-Fi hotspots fill in the gaps away from the home and office. They allow people to keep up-to-date with their digital world wherever a hotspot might be, whether it is in an airport, café, restaurant, or hotel.

Installing and operating your own Wi-Fi hotspot at your business or organization allows you to be a part of this rapidly growing technology. Even installing a small wireless network has proven to be a difficult task for the average consumer. With this book acting as your guide, you can painlessly figure out what is required for your Wi-Fi hotspot, how to properly set it up, and how to operate it.

Goal and Method

The goal of this book is to help people, such as small business or location owners, set up a Wi-Fi hotspot to offer free or fee-based Internet access to the public. Not only does this book offer valuable tips on installing Wi-Fi hotspots, but it also walks you through four different hotspot solutions. The step-by-step procedures used in the solutions simplify the process of setting up a hotspot and ensure that you always know what you need to do.

This book provides information in a simple manner so that even nontechnical consumers can understand the necessary technical information to set up a Wi-Fi hotspot.

Who Should Read This Book?

Anyone from IT professionals to self-proclaimed computer illiterates who are involved with the installation, administration, or support of a Wi-Fi hotspot should read this book.

How This Book Is Organized

Although this book is organized well, you should follow the flow to ensure that you get the best out of this book.

- **Part I, "The Basics"**
- **Chapter 1, "The Basics of Wi-Fi Hotspots"**—This chapter heightens your understanding of Wi-Fi hotspots and how they fit into everyday life. It serves as an introduction to hotspots to ensure that you have a basic understanding before you proceed with installing your own.
- **Chapter 2, "The Business Side of Hosting a Hotspot"**—This chapter explains the benefits of hosting a hotspot, including generating additional revenue and attracting more people to your business or organization. This chapter helps you decide which type of hotspot you should implement by factoring in the associated costs, revenue, and benefits.

- **Chapter 3, "First Steps to Setting Up a Wi-Fi Hotspot"**—This chapter explains the overall steps of setting up your Wi-Fi hotspot so that you know exactly what to do. You get started with Steps 1 and 2, learning about the specific hotspot solutions that are covered in this book and picking one based on your situation. Then you learn about the different Internet connections and which types are best for your hotspot.

- **Part II, "Setting Up the Hotspot" (Chapters 4–7)**—The chapters in Part II cover the specific hotspot solutions discussed. Each chapter contains step-by-step instructions to set up the solutions to cover a small area, such as a café or lobby. If you are not satisfied with the coverage area after completing the initial setup, or if your plans are to cover a large area, such as a hotel or motel, you should refer to Chapter 12 after completing one of these solutions.

- **Part III: After Your Wi-Fi Hotspot Is Alive**

- **Chapter 8, "Getting the Word Out"**—This chapter discusses how to get the word out about your Wi-Fi hotspot so that you can start attracting more people to your business or organization.

- **Chapter 9, "Fending Off Freeloaders"**—This chapter explains how people can take advantage of free wireless Internet access and gives you ways to fend them off to ensure that your Wi-Fi hotspot is not used improperly.

- **Chapter 10, "Wi-Fi Security"**—This chapter covers security issues relating to Wi-Fi hotspots. Hotspots cannot be secured like homes and businesses, because they are for public use. You learn what you need to know to ensure that everyone has a good hotspot experience.

- **Chapter 11, "Common Problems and Fixes"**—This chapter explains common problems you or your users might experience while using your hotspot and steps to take to fix them.

- **Chapter 12, "Increasing Your Hotspot's Wireless Coverage"**—This chapter introduces you to a few ways that you can increase the coverage area of your new or existing Wi-Fi hotspot and step-by-step instructions for each method.

- **Chapter 13, "Using Wi-Fi Networks"**—This chapter contains step-by-step procedures for common tasks when using Wi-Fi networks. If you are new to using wireless networks, this chapter enables you to use your Wi-Fi hotspot by teaching you the basics, such as connecting and sharing files.

- **Appendix A, "Understanding Wi-Fi Signals"**—The appendix discuses many topics; such as wireless signals and interference, which helps you during the installation and administration of your Wi-Fi hotspot. This information also instills you with some common sense that's helpful when dealing with problems that may arise.

Part I: **The Basics**

Chapter 1   The Basics of Wi-Fi Hotspots

Chapter 2   The Business Side of Hosting a Hotspot

Chapter 3   First Steps to Setting Up a Wi-Fi Hotspot

Chapter 1

The Basics of Wi-Fi Hotspots

Wi-Fi hotspots provide wireless Internet access within public areas. They enable people to keep up-to-date with their digital world in places such as cafés (as depicted in Figure 1-1), convention centers, libraries, and hotels. Users can connect to hotspots from mobile computers, such as laptops and Personal Digital Assistants (PDAs). Other media devices with Wi-Fi capability, such as the PlayStation Portable (PSP) or cellular phones, can also take advantage of hotspots. Wireless hotspots allow people to do such tasks as browse the Internet and send and receive e-mail. Wi-Fi hotspots are similar to wireless networks that are used in homes and businesses; however, they are not as secure, and they are intended for public use.

Figure 1-1   Wi-Fi Hotspot User in a Café

Hotspots provide *broadband*, or high-speed, Internet access. This type of connection is much faster than traditional Internet connections, such as dialup access using a telephone modem. However, the Internet speed that individual users experience while connected to a wireless network varies, depending on many factors, including the following:

- The size and configuration of the hotspot
- The number of concurrent users
- What the users are doing on the network

For example, the Internet speed for individual users on a hotspot might be faster if a few people are synchronizing e-mail, rather than a dozen users downloading large files or viewing streaming video on a website.

NOTE A broadband Internet connection can support up to a 4500-kilobits per second (kbps) transfer rate. These Internet connections are much faster than what traditional 56-kbps telephone dialup modems provide. This speeds up web browsing and downloading for users.

Many types of hotspots exist throughout the world. Traditional hotspots provide coverage in and around a building or small group of buildings, such as restaurants, coffee shops, airports, and hotels. Access to hotspots can be free or fee-based. Even if Internet access on a hotspot is free, users might be required to register or view advertisements before accessing the Internet. Fee-based hotspots require users to register and purchase access time. These rates and times differ between each hotspot network. A typical hotspot network might have an access fee selection such as $6 for an hour of access, $10 for 24 hours, and $30 for unlimited access for a month. As discussed in the following case study, hotspots can be independent or part of a network or group.

Hotspot Networks Versus Independent Hotspots

Jared is a regular McDonald's customer; he typically stops by in the morning, eats breakfast, and reviews his college assignments on a laptop. After seeing a sign advertising the McDonald's Internet hotspot, he decides to purchase a monthly access plan so that he can browse the Internet while at McDonald's. He likes to read the news on Google and catch up on e-mail with his friends. During the signup process, he learns that he can use the same username and password at any McDonald's Wi-Fi hotspot location, rather than just at his hometown store. Even more exciting, Jared finds out that the McDonald's hotspot belongs to a large hotspot network called Wayport. As a result, he also can use thousands of other Wayport hotspots at non-McDonald's locations.

If the hotspot were independent—not part of other McDonald's stores and Wayport hotspots—Jared would not have the potential to use those thousands of hotspots. He would be paying to access the hotspot of just that single store.

E-mail and web browsing are available through most mobile phone service providers. However, these phones have limited keypads and displays. Devices such as the Blackberry offer quick and simple e-mail access and have had great success in the market. However, creating or viewing larger e-mail messages and viewing most websites are not practical. In addition, the data rates available through the cell systems are relatively slow. Therefore, people who have laptops and PDAs equipped with

Wi-Fi connectivity can benefit much more by connecting to the Internet via a Wi-Fi hotspot, which offers a more effective user interface and much higher speed.

Most hotspots display a splash screen the first time a user connects and accesses the Internet with a web browser. With free hotspots, this splash screen might require the user just to accept terms and conditions (the "fine print") or view advertisements before accessing the Internet connection. If the hotspot is fee-based, a user would enter his logon information or sign up and set up payments if he has not used that hotspot network before. In most cases, the fee-based hotspots accept payments by having the user securely enter credit card information.

Bridging the Gap

Wi-Fi hotspots bridge the Wi-Fi connectivity gap between wireless networks in homes and businesses. People can access e-mail and other online services between home and work or while traveling. This allows them to keep up with customers, associates, and family members.

A Typical Hotspot User

Imagine that Denise sits at the kitchen table at breakfast and reads the news on her favorite website before heading to work in the morning. She corresponds often with her family and friends via instant messaging or e-mail; however, she cannot do this while at work. The management does not allow use of their wireless network or company computers for personal reasons. Therefore, she takes along her laptop when visiting a favorite café during lunch breaks. She grabs a bite to eat, chats with friends online, and responds to e-mails. This keeps her in touch with others while not breaking rules at work.

Wi-Fi hotspots are found in many public places where people might want to pop open their laptop and browse the Internet. Following are some typical places where you might find a Wi-Fi hotspot:

- Cafés, restaurants, and bars
- Hotels, motels, and bed-and-breakfast inns
- Bookstores and libraries
- Office building reception areas
- Airports
- Airplanes
- Clubs and organizations

As discussed in the preceeding case study, cafés and restaurants provide wireless Internet access for customers while they are enjoying their food and beverages. Along with other businesses and organizations, cafés and restaurants will likely benefit with more foot traffic to their location when they provide this convenient Internet service to customers and visitors.

A majority of travelers these days choose only hotels that provide broadband Internet access within the rooms. This lets people keep in touch with their online world while they are out of town. Some hotels provide a wired Internet connection—usually an Ethernet or data port. Ethernet provides broadband Internet access similar to Wi-Fi, but Ethernet requires a cable to connect the user laptop to the network. This restricts the user to a single location in the room—usually a desk. In addition, most hotels provide a data port on the telephone for dialup modem users to plug into. This also requires a restrictive cable connection, and the performance is slow and unusable for some websites and e-mail attachment downloads.

Even though wired Internet connections are widely available, most people prefer Wi-Fi Internet access. This enables guests to move about the hotel and still be connected to the Internet. For example, a business traveler can use the Internet from anywhere within the room, such as from the desk, as shown in Figure 1-2, or while relaxing on the bed. In addition, this person can go down to the bar or lobby and still have Internet access. A Wi-Fi network in a hotel also becomes useful when one or more people with laptops are staying in the same room, because wired connections allow only one person at a time to use the Internet.

Figure 1-2   Hotspot User in a Hotel Room

Students, businesspeople, and others typically use Wi-Fi hotspots at local bookstores and libraries while working on homework or work-related tasks. Bookstores typically did not have Internet access before they began offering Wi-Fi access. For years, libraries have had computer workstations connected to the Internet for public use.

Yet offering Wi-Fi Internet access helps eliminate some costs, enables more people to use the Internet at once, and lets users move about the building while using Internet applications.

Corporations in the past did not have Internet access available for visitors throughout their office buildings because of the difficulties in allocating a wired connection. In most cases, an unused wired Ethernet port is not available or is in a physical location where it is not practical for the visitor to access it. An open port, for example, could be located on the wall within the conference room. Regularly scheduled meetings in the conference room would likely get in the way of the visitor using the room to use the network connection. Visitors such as salespeople, customers, and consultants, though, can definitely benefit from Wi-Fi Internet access while inside the facility, even if the wireless network is made available only from specific places, such as the company lobby, and kept separate from the corporate network.

Wi-Fi Internet access within airports enables travelers, such as shown in Figure 1-3, to send and receive e-mail and conduct other necessary tasks while traveling. This is useful during long layovers between flights and unscheduled delays or cancellations. Many airports today still have not installed wireless hotspots. Given that airports can be extremely large, this could be an expensive task for the airport authorities. However, even installing a small hotspot within specific restaurants, airline clubs, or concourses of the airport would be useful to travelers.

Figure 1-3   Hotspot User in an Airport

Wi-Fi access is also available while onboard aircraft during some international airline flights. The Federal Aviation Administration (FAA) at the time of this writing prevents airlines that are flying domestically in the United States from offering Wi-Fi on airplanes, however. When Internet access on airplanes becomes widely accepted, many people will benefit, especially during longer flights. Business travelers will certainly be more productive if they can correspond via e-mail and use Internet-based applications while they are restricted to an airplane seat.

Many businesses today, such as those discussed in the preceding paragraphs, are setting up hotspots throughout all their locations, or franchisees. Table 1-1 lists a few examples.

Table 1-1   *Companies That Provide Wi-Fi Hotspots*

Company	Type	Hotspot Network
Starbucks coffee shops	Fee	T-Mobile
McDonald's fast food restaurants	Fee	Wayport (U.S.)
Panera Bread cafés	Free	—
Marriot hotels	Fee	Boingo

Wi-Fi Hot Zones

Wi-Fi hot zones, also known as *Wi-Fi clouds*, provide public Internet access, just like hotspots, but they cover a larger area, such as that shown in Figure 1-4, and they are typically for use outdoors. These hot zones might cover anywhere from a city block to an entire city, commonly referred to as a *muni* or *municipal network*, or even a whole county.

Even though end users in these hot zones connect using Wi-Fi, these systems typically use a different design approach, called *mesh networking*, instead of the traditional wireless LAN infrastructure, such as in Wi-Fi hotspots.

Along with giving citizens and visitors convenient Internet access, these wireless networks might provide a concurrent private network and Internet connections over the same system. Companies might be able to purchase a secure Internet connection for their business, and city departments could support communication services such as parking and utility meters and city cameras.

Figure 1-4   View of Hot Zone Coverage

NOTE   Larger wireless networks such as city-wide or corporate networks provide private and public access simultaneously by using VLANs. VLANs provide secure and logical separation for both the private and public network users while requiring only one physical network infrastructure.

Following is a short list of the cities that are filling the streets with Wi-Fi signals:

- Tulsa, Oklahoma
- Cape Cod, Massachusetts
- Sunnyvale, California
- Daytona Beach and Panama City, Florida

More and more cities are hopping on the muni Wi-Fi bandwagon, trying to keep up with the digital world and wanting to attract people and businesses to their area.

These hot zones are convenient, allowing people to check their e-mail and browse the Internet pretty much anywhere outdoors within the coverage area. In some cases, users can even access the Internet in moving vehicles, where traditional hotspots do not cover.

 NOTE Even though metropolitan Wi-Fi networks are getting popular, traditional small hotspots will always be important, especially in towns where muni access is not available. Even in cities that have municipal Wi-Fi networks, the lack of coverage within buildings and the inability to provide perfect connections to users from every nook and cranny ensures that certain people will need and use traditional small hotspots.

How Users Find Hotspots

People find hotspots in many different ways:

- Online directories
- Software directories
- Display signs
- Wi-Fi finders
- Laptops/PDAs

People who want Internet access while traveling can find hotspots in particular areas by searching online directories. They can view pertinent details of the hotspots, such as the service set identifier (SSID), also referred to as the hotspot's *network name*, and whether the network is free or fee-based. The following are a few websites offering online directories that people can use to find hotspots:

- www.jiwire.com/
- www.wi-fihotspotlist.com/
- www.wifinder.com/
- www.hotspot-locations.com/

Many of the major hotspot networks and online directories also offer a free software program that people can download and install on their computers. This allows travelers who are on the go—even in the car or airport—to quickly find hotspots without an Internet connection. Following are a few websites that offer offline or downloadable software directories:

- www.jiwire.com/
- www.boingo.com/
- hotspot.t-mobile.com/

Many businesses and organizations display signs throughout their facility indicating that they host a public hotspot. The display of door, counter, and street signs helps notify people passing by or through the location of the Wi-Fi hotspot.

Figure 1-5 shows a typical device called a Wi-Fi finder, which provides a way for gadget lovers to find hotspots. This immediately lets someone know if a wireless network is nearby, without the hassle of the user taking out and booting up his laptop. The features and functionality of these devices differ greatly, depending on the manufacturer. Some finders notify the user of Wi-Fi networks just by illuminating a certain light. More advanced finders might have a small screen that displays important information about the detected network, such as the SSID, security level, and signal strength.

Figure 1-5   Example of a Wi-Fi Finder

Wi-Fi finders are convenient; however, they might notify you of every wireless network nearby, not just the public hotspots. Wireless networks that are intended for private use can be secured so that the public cannot connect. Nevertheless, a good percentage of businesses and consumers do not fully understand the security risks and do not properly secure their network. If a private wireless network is not properly secured, anybody can potentially connect and access the Internet and files on the network. Thus, some people think that just because they can connect to a network, it is a hotspot and it is open to the public. Instead, some of these Wi-Fi networks belong to private citizens and businesses. They might not be intended for public use and might even be unlawful to use.

NOTE   If you are unsure whether a certain wireless network is a public hotspot, you should find the network's owner and ask, because that is the only way to be certain.

Many people find Wi-Fi hotspots simply by booting up their laptop or PDA and viewing the available wireless networks in the area. This also brings up the issue that some networks might not be intended for public use. Users should look for networks that are clearly identified for public use.

How Wi-Fi Works

Wireless networks use a technology that is specified within a standard called 802.11. The standard is basically written documents formed by members of the IEEE. These documents help manufacturers develop wireless products so that they will work together with wireless products from every vendor that follows the standard.

The 802.11 standard has a few versions:

- 802.11a
- 802.11b
- 802.11g

These versions of 802.11 have different characteristics, such as data rate, frequency, and transmit power limits. The most widely used standard today is 802.11g, which is similar to 802.11b. However, it can handle a much greater data rate, up to 54 Mbps. The details of these standards are discussed in Appendix A, "Understanding Wi-Fi Signals."

The word "Wi-Fi" that is used throughout the market was created by the Wi-Fi Alliance, a nonprofit industry trade association devoted to promoting the growth of wireless local-area networks (WLAN). The Wi-Fi Alliance certifies products to ensure the interoperability of WLAN products from different manufacturers and try to promote the use of these devices. The Alliance defines the word "Wi-Fi" as follows:

A term developed by the Wi-Fi Alliance to describe wireless local-area network (WLAN) products that are based on the IEEE 802.11 standards.

NOTE   The Wi-Fi Alliance was originally called the Wireless Ethernet Compatibility Alliance (WECA).

Other people describe the term "Wi-Fi" as *wireless fidelity*, or freedom from wires.

Most wireless networks operate in a similar way, regardless of whether it is a private or public network. Cities, however, typically use mesh networking technology to help simplify the installation and operation of such a large network. Smaller hotspots use an infrastructure that is similar to wireless networks in homes and businesses.

The three main components of infrastructure wireless networks are as follows:

- Internet service
- Internet modem
- Wireless router

Figure 1-6 shows a simple layout of a Wi-Fi network. This is not necessarily how a hotspot or any specific network is set up. It merely shows a basic configuration of a wireless network.

Figure 1-6   Layout of a Basic Wi-Fi Network

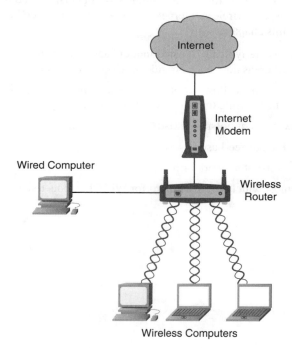

Of course, to provide wireless Internet to users, you must have some type of Internet service connected to the network. Most Internet service providers (ISPs) supply a modem and usually hook it up for you. The Internet modem physically connects to the Internet line (as shown in Figure 1-6), such as a DSL or TV cable jack.

The wireless router (as shown in Figure 1-6) takes a single Internet connection and distributes usage among wired and wireless users on the network. All wireless devices on the network communicate through the wireless router. It is the controller and coordinator for all the wireless traffic.

NOTE Wireless networks that need to cover an area beyond that of a single wireless router use multiple access points instead of wireless routers. Only one device on the network needs the ability to route and regulate traffic on the network. Therefore, larger networks have many access points that do not have routing features, connected to a separate piece of hardware that does the routing.

Chapter Review

This chapter discussed that the intention of Wi-Fi hotspots and hot zones is to give the public high-speed wireless Internet access. In addition, keep in mind the main points covered in this chapter:

- Hotspots are typically located indoors and provide a relatively small coverage area, whereas hot zones provide access outside over a much larger area.

- Wi-Fi hotspots allow people to check e-mail, surf the web, and perform other online tasks while they are away from home or work.

- A few types of hotspots exist:
  — Free or fee-based
  — Hotspot network or independent

- The most widely used standard for Wi-Fi hotspots today is 802.11g.

Chapter 2

The Business Side of Hosting a Hotspot

In this chapter, you will learn about the benefits of hosting a hotspot, such as generating additional revenue and attracting more people to your business or organization, and the associated costs of doing so. This will help you decide which type of hotspot is best for your particular situation.

Benefits of Hosting a Wi-Fi Hotspot

The overall benefit or goal of hosting a Wi-Fi hotspot at your location is being able to offer high-speed wireless Internet access there. In addition to satisfying the needs of connectivity for your customers and visitors, you and your staff can take advantage of having the Internet readily available.

Other benefits of hosting a Wi-Fi hotspot include these:

- Attract people to your location
- Generate additional revenue
- Create a private network for your own use

Attract People to Your Location

Hosting a Wi-Fi hotspot, in any type of business, should attract new people to your location and entice them to return and stay longer. For retail stores such as cafés and bookstores, this access helps fill empty seats. For businesses such as hotels, having Wi-Fi Internet access available for guests might be essential to prevent losing potential customers.

As discussed earlier, people find hotspots in many ways, including these:

- Online directories
- Software directories
- Display signs
- Wi-Fi finders
- Laptop/PDAs

Obviously, for people to find your hotspot in directories, you must submit your information. If you set up your hotspot to be part of a network such as Boingo or T-Mobile, your information would likely be listed automatically in their directories. You can also submit your hotspot to universal directories that list any hotspot, free or fee-based, whether it is independent or part of a larger network.

The best way to attract users to your hotspot is to display signs advertising that you have a hotspot at your location. These signs could simply say "Wi-Fi Hotspot Here" or "Wireless Internet Access Available."

Brian Searches for Wi-Fi Hotspots

Brian, a college student, is planning his trip to New York City for a three-week co-op job. At home and school, he uses his laptop to access the Internet to research topics, write papers, and keep in touch with family and friends. He wants to be able to have the Internet readily available during his entire stay in New York.

He starts by finding hotels with Wi-Fi Internet access. After searching travel websites and hotspot directories, Brian finds a hotel that offers complimentary Wi-Fi access in the rooms and within the outdoor courtyard. He decides to book this hotel.

Brian also enjoys doing homework at hometown cafés and coffee shops. Therefore, before leaving home, he wants to find a few places around the hotel and job location where he can grab a bite to eat and surf the web. After a few minutes of searching hotspot directories, he finds three interesting cafés he wants to try.

After Brian arrived in New York, he soon found many more hotspots at other cafés and bookstores that were not listed in the directories. He simply saw the "hotspot here" signs hanging in windows as he walked to his co-op job.

After stepping you through installing and setting up your wireless network, Chapter 8, "Getting the Word Out," further discusses how to advertise your hotspot.

Generate Additional Revenue

While you are providing a convenient service to your customers and visitors by hosting a Wi-Fi hotspot, you might also generate some additional revenue for your business or organization. Here are ways that you can create some revenue:

- Indirect sales of your products or services
- Hotspot network commissions
- Fees from an independent fee-based hotspot
- Advertising revenue

Increased Sales of Products or Services

As mentioned numerous times earlier, hosting a Wi-Fi hotspot will likely attract many new visitors to your location. Getting more people in a store and enticing them to stay longer usually means you will sell more of your products or services. Thus, you should see increased revenue while hosting a wireless hotspot.

Estimating this potential indirect revenue is difficult for any business or organization. To start, ask yourself a few questions based on your particular situation:

- **Are your current customers or visitors the type who would sit at your location with a laptop and check e-mail or browse the Internet?**—If your answer is yes or even maybe, the hotspot will likely attract people. If the answer is absolutely no, you probably should not be taking all this time to set up a hotspot that no one would likely use.

- **How many people do you think this hotspot would attract?**—You should estimate the number of people, per month, that you think would visit your location just because of your Wi-Fi hotspot. Start by thinking about how many customers or orders you currently receive, and then estimate additional numbers.

- **Will hotspot users buy products and services?**—You could rely on most of the hotspot users to purchase products or services. If your hotspot will be fee-based, you do not need to worry about this as much, because you will be paid through hotspot usage. When it comes to giving away free access, you probably want only paying customers or members of your organization to use your hotspot. For instance, in businesses such as cafés and restaurants, it is usually socially incorrect for noncustomers to use their restrooms. Therefore, people who use your free Wi-Fi hotspot will likely purchase your products or services.

- **How much will your revenue increase by hosting a hotspot?**—By using information about your business or organization, estimate how much revenue you can gain from having a hotspot at your location. See the following case study for some ideas that will aid you in the process.

Sam's Coffee Shop—Estimating Indirect Revenue

Sam is pretty sure he wants to set up a Wi-Fi hotspot in his coffee shop; however, he wants to weigh the benefits and costs to ensure that this is a task he wants to take on.

First, he wants to get an idea of how much this hotspot will help increase the primary sales of his business, which is coffee and snacks. Because this matters more if access is free, he will use that scenario when estimating the indirect revenue.

Given that most of his customers, especially in the mornings, are local businesspeople, he believes they would be the type who would use their laptops and PDAs at his store.

Next, he needs to estimate the number of people the hotspot would attract. He gets an average of 3000 orders per month at his coffee shop. He estimates about 5 percent (150) of new orders each month, or five per day, will be because the people noticed the store had free wireless Internet access. This seems fairly reasonable.

He then figures that about 75 percent of those visitors would purchase coffee or a snack while taking advantage of the Wi-Fi hotspot. Using the math shown next, he figures about 113 orders will be because the person was attracted to his store by the hotspot.

With an average purchase per order of $8, Sam can then estimate how much more revenue his store would produce by having a hotspot:

$8 average purchase × 113 new visitors per month = $904 *revenue* gain per month

The math shows that just by having the hotspot, Sam will gain about $904 of sales in a month, increasing his revenue by about 4 percent:

3000 orders × $8 average purchase = $24,000 per month revenues

$904 revenue gain ÷ $24,000 current revenue = 3.7 percent revenue increase

Sam is happy with the estimate and thinks that his business will continually do better with the hotspot, even by offering free Wi-Fi service. The new visitors brought in by the hotspot will likely become repeat customers.

Hotspot Network Commissions

Keep in mind that when hosting a fee-based hotspot, you obviously have the potential to earn more direct revenue from the hotspot than if you were giving away free access. If you team up with a hotspot network such as Boingo, you will receive commissions. However, also consider that when hosting a fee-based hotspot, you typically will receive fewer users than if you were to host a free hotspot.

When you collaborate with a hotspot network, such as Boingo, it takes care of all the payments from users; you just sit back and wait for people to connect to your hotspot. Boingo keeps track of everything.

As of this writing, here is the commission structure that Boingo offers its hotspot partners:

- Connect commissions:
  - $1.00 per connect day for monthly subscribers
  - $4.00 per connect day for "as you go" users
- Sign-up commissions:
  - $20.00 per sign-up for a monthly subscription

Boingo charges hotspot users $21.95 per month for unlimited access, with no contract required. These subscribers have access to more than 25,000 hotspots worldwide, in addition to one you might deploy. Boingo also offers people a 24-hour access period for a single hotspot, at $9.95. These people are called "as you go" users.

In addition to the connect fees, you would earn $20.00 every time a new customer signed up for the monthly subscription. The only requirement is that the subscription must last more than 60 days.

Now you should determine the amount of money you think you would receive each month from Boingo. See the following case study for some ideas.

Sam's Coffee Shop—Estimating Revenue from Boingo

Sam is not sure which type of hotspot he wants to set up at his coffee shop, so he thinks about each situation. To determine whether he wants to go the Boingo route, he estimates how much commission he thinks the hotspot would generate. His coffee shop is located downtown in a large city, and most of his customers are businesspeople. Thus, he figures he will receive a minimum of 100 connections each month to the Boingo hotspot, or about four per weekday. He estimates 80 people each month will be monthly subscribers, and the other 20 people will be "as you go" users. Following is the math, depicting the money Sam might receive just from connect commissions:

$4.00 × 20 "as you go" connections = $80

$1.00 × 80 monthly subscriber connections = $80

$80 + $80 = $160 of estimated connect commissions per month

Sam then projects that he will receive credit for having about eight people each month sign up for the Boingo monthly service through his location:

$20 × 8 sign-ups = $160 estimated sign-up commissions per month

Sam is happy with the final estimate: $320 of direct revenue. With this amount, he could easily recoup the equipment and associated costs of setting up the hotspot within a month or two. In addition, the advertising of a Wi-Fi hotspot, even though it is fee-based, will attract new customers to his store who will purchase more coffee and snacks. Nevertheless, he keeps his options open, because he is not sure what will happen.

Fees from an Independent Fee-Based Hotspot

If you will host a fee-based hotspot independently, without the help of a hotspot network like Boingo, you need to define your own pricing and terms. To help figure this out, refer to what others are doing. However, remember that because your hotspot is independent, people who join it will not receive the same benefits as if they were to join a network like Boingo. Big hotspot networks like Boingo have many more locations where users can connect under a single subscription. The user's ability to roam and the number of hotspots within the network should be one of the main factors you consider when determining your hotspot pricing and terms. The following case study gives you an idea of how to determine pricing for an independent fee-based hotspot.

Sam's Coffee Shop—Estimating Revenue from an Independent Fee-Based Hotspot

Sam now needs to estimate the revenue he could produce if he were to set up an independent fee-based hotspot at his downtown coffee shop. The first task is to come up with a feasible fee structure for the prospective users. Because the users will be paying just for the use of his hotspot, he does not think that offering a monthly subscription is practical. On the other hand, Sam thinks that he will have a better chance of getting per-day and per-hour users because networks like Boingo also limit the use of a single hotspot when you pay for a 24-hour access period. He will base his predictions on the following rates:

$4 for an hour

$10 for 24 hours

Sam figures that he will receive a minimum of 80 total connections to his hotspot in a month. This number is less than his estimate with the Boingo hotspot, as discussed in an earlier case study, because his hotspot would not belong to a large network, which would likely attract more visitors. He estimates that the independent hotspot will have 65 one-hour connections and 15 24-hour connections each month.

$4 × 65 1-hour connections = $260

$10 × 15 24-hour connections = $150

His math shows estimated direct revenue of $410 if he goes the independent fee-based route.

After comparing the two fee-based hotspot types—Boingo and an independent hotspot—Sam leans toward the independent hotspot because of the higher revenue estimate. However, he is cautious because it seems a bit harder to set up his own fee-based hotspot than it is to join the Boingo network.

Advertising Revenue

You can still make some direct revenue from hosting a free-access hotspot by selling advertising. The advertisements could be placed on the splash screen web page, which users would see at least the first time they connect, per session. Selling advertising is not recommended for everyone, because it can be time-consuming to make deals with local businesses and to set up the advertisements on your hotspot.

If you think you will be accepting advertisements, you need to think about pricing and terms for potential advertisers. Then come up with a ballpark figure of the potential revenue your business could generate from these advertisements.

Sam's Coffee Shop—Thinking About Selling Advertising

Sam would really like to give his customers free Wi-Fi Internet access; however, he does not want to pay for the equipment and monthly Internet connection. Thus, he will look into selling advertising to help recoup the hotspot's operating costs. Table 2-1 shows a rough idea of how much Sam anticipates charging for the advertisements based on the number of connections his hotspot receives in a month.

Table 2-1   *Sam's Hotspot Advertising Pricing*

Users	Fee
< 100	$25
101–200	$50
200 >	$75

Sam will use the pricing from his early estimate of 150 people who would use a free Wi-Fi hotspot at his coffee shop. Assuming after a while that he picks up four businesses that are willing to advertise to his hotspot users, he comes up with the estimated monthly revenue for selling advertising:

$50 × 4 advertisers = $200

These calculations make him feel much better about hosting a free hotspot. He would have to spend some time creating terms and learning how to place the advertisement images on the splash screen. However, the monthly income of $200 from advertising and $904 in estimated increased revenue (see the earlier case study) make it well worth the costs of installing a Wi-Fi hotspot.

Ability to Create a Private Network

After setting up a Wi-Fi hotspot, you can easily create a private wired or wireless network for use by you and your employees. The private and public networks can share the same Internet connection. Of course, this will not concern you if you already have a private network set up at the hotspot location. In this case, you can share the existing Internet connection between the private and public networks. If set up correctly, the private and public networks will be independent of each other, and your private network will be secured from the public.

Setting up your own private wireless network for your business or organization has the following benefits:

- Mobility
- Secure Internet browsing
- Shared files and printers
- Use of wireless devices, such as the following:
    - Media adapters
    - Presentation adapters
    - Wi-Fi video cams
    - Print servers

Just like Wi-Fi hotspots, having a wireless network for your business enables you to have mobility when using laptops and other Wi-Fi devices. You can access the Internet and print documents from anywhere within your facility. In addition, with Wi-Fi, you can move your desktop PCs anywhere within the coverage area, without the hassle of running ugly telephone or Ethernet cabling throughout the office.

You could use your own Wi-Fi hotspot to browse the Internet and perform online tasks. However, unlike private networks, Wi-Fi hotspots must be left unencrypted and unsecured so that the public can effortlessly connect to the hotspot. Anyone who has the right software and tools can see what you and others are doing on the web. People can also see passwords for services like FTP and POP3 e-mail. If sharing services are set up on your computer, people might also be able to browse your files and get into your computer.

 CAUTION   Make sure you thoroughly understand the consequences of using an unsecured wireless network, such as a hotspot, before conducting important tasks.

On the other hand, people cannot easily see information being passed to and from secured websites such as online online banking and shopping carts, which normally use Secure Sockets Layer (SSL) encryption. As shown in Figure 2-1, Internet Explorer and other web browsers let you know if the website is using SSL encryption by displaying a padlock. Another hint is that websites protected with this technology usually start with https: instead of the regular http:

TIP   Along with a variety of other tools and methods, you can use virtual private network (VPN) connections to help secure the data that is passing to and from your computer. This is a great way to temporarily protect your data while surfing the web on a hotspot.

Figure 2-1   Example of an SSL Indicator

When your computers are on their own private network, you can securely use file and service sharing. Windows XP has built-in features that enable you to easily drag and drop files to and from the computers on your network. Windows XP also supports printer sharing. Without other devices, you can hook a printer to just one computer, and all the PCs on the network can use it, too.

Many Wi-Fi accessories are available that do some pretty neat things, and they are useful in many businesses and organizations. Again, you could supposedly use these accessories on your public hotspot, but the data would not be protected.

Wireless media adapters, such as the one shown in Figure 2-2, also called Wireless Media Players or Entertainment Center Extenders, can stream digital audio and video files from computers on the network to your TV and stereo. In a corporate setting, this is a great way to display your company logos, photos, and slide shows to customers and visitors. In cafés, you can use the remote control of the media adapter to browse and choose your media files, all from a TV. Some even support Internet radio, giving you a chance to listen in on a variety of music from around the world.

Figure 2-2   Linksys Wireless A/G Media Center Extender—WMCE54AG

Wireless presentation players, such as the one pictured in Figure 2-3, are extremely valuable for interactive presentations and conferences. One of the simpler advantages of this device is that it enables you to wirelessly connect to a projector or monitor from your computer to display to everyone your computer screen or your presentation. Some presentation players might even allow other wireless users to connect to the device and take over the presentation or display their screen on the monitor. This allows a group of people to quickly and clearly share their ideas and notes. With internal memory or removable storage, such as a USB flash drive, you could load the PowerPoint or other presentation files onto the player and make a presentation without a computer.

Figure 2-3   Linksys Wireless-G Presentation Player—WPG54G

Wireless video cameras, such as the one shown in Figure 2-4, are useful for video-conferencing and surveillance. You and other authorized users can "see what it sees and hear what it hears" from anywhere in the world via the Internet. Most cameras have a motion detection feature, which sends you an e-mail when the camera view experiences activity. Some Wi-Fi cameras even have a remote-control feature whereby you can change the camera view using its web-based utility. The quality of these Wi-Fi cameras differs greatly among manufacturers. Among other accessories, vendors might offer outdoor and ceiling enclosures for their cameras.

Figure 2-4 Linksys Wireless-G Internet Video Camera—WVC54G

Figuring the Costs

Hosting a hotspot does not come cheap, yet the benefits usually outweigh the costs. Typical operating costs you should anticipate while installing and hosting your Wi-Fi hotspot are as follows:

- **Internet service**—$60 or more per month
- **Equipment**—$40–$500 one time
- **Installation**—1–2 days of your time
- **Ongoing support**—A few hours each month

If you do not already have an Internet connection available for the hotspot, that will be one of your first expenses. Business-class Internet service prices and terms depend on the type of service and features among the various ISPs.

If you are deploying a small hotspot, as in a small café or bookstore that will not have loads of users, you will likely get away with paying $35–$80 per month for an Internet connection. However, if you are setting up a hotspot in a large hotel or library, you will probably have a great deal of users, which would require a higher-quality Internet connection that might cost $100 to $300 a month. Chapter 3, "First Steps to Setting Up a Wi-Fi Hotspot," further discusses the Internet connection types.

The cost of the equipment, or hardware, varies significantly depending on the size and type of hotspot you plan to install.

The simplest hotspot using the same type of wireless router that is used in homes will cost only around $40. This type of hotspot is simple because it has no hotspot features such as user redirection, usage limits, required login, and so on. However, this book presents a scenario in which you can use free software to get these hotspot features at no cost, making an affordable hotspot solution if you have an extra PC available. However, you still have to purchase some equipment to use in conjunction with the free software. Factor in about $50 for this equipment when you are installing a small hotspot.

Installing a Wi-Fi hotspot to provide coverage for a large area, such as an entire library or hotel, might cost up to $1500 or more, depending on the number of access points that are needed to cover the area.

Although your time might not be a direct cost, your time is probably valuable. If it helps, you can assign a cost to the time you will spend installing and supporting your hotspot. Of course, you can always use evenings and weekends to install the system to avoid impacting your business.

The time involved in installing a hotspot also depends on the solution's size and complexity. This could take just an hour for a simple setup of a single wireless router covering a small area or several days to cover an entire building.

Keep in mind that you have to take time to support your hotspot. You never know when problems will pop up, whether someone will mistakenly unplug the wireless router or not know how to connect to the network. You might find yourself spending a few hours each month supporting your hotspot. In addition, you might need to spend some time upfront learning about how Wi-Fi works to effectively support your customers.

Sam's Coffee Shop—Figuring the Costs

Sam needs to estimate the costs of hosting a hotspot in his coffee shop. He comes up with the following:

Internet service—$55 per month

Equipment—$50

He has not researched the exact prices for business-class Internet service in his area, but he thinks it will be about $55 per month, within the range $35–$80 discussed earlier. He is thinking about using the free-software scenario, so he estimates only $50 for the equipment.

Sam's Coffee Shop—Free or Fee-Based?

To get a better idea of which type of hotspot Sam wants to put in his coffee shop, he summarizes the estimated revenue and costs:

Benefits:

- Indirect revenue—$904 per month
- Revenue from Boingo—$320 per month
- Independent fee-based hotspot—$410 per month

Costs:

- Internet service—$55 per month
- Equipment—$50

Sam quickly sees that he could make some fairly nice profits. He thinks it would be nice to make the estimated $300–$500 per month from the fee-based hotspots; however, he would really like to offer free access to better compete with the restaurants and cafés in the area.

After doing some thinking and talking with his employees and regular customers, he decides that offering free access to his hotspot would be the best situation.

Chapter Review

Now you should have a better feeling of the benefits and costs that are associated with hosting a Wi-Fi hotspot and which type you want to implement.

Remember the main benefits of hosting a hotspot:

- Providing wireless Internet access for your visitors
- Attracting people to your location
- Generating additional revenue
- Creating a private network for your own use

In addition, do not forget the costs:

- Internet service—$60 or more per month
- Equipment—$40–$500 one time
- Installation—1–2 days of your time
- Ongoing support—A few hours each month

Chapter 3

First Steps to Setting Up a Wi-Fi Hotspot

The following are the overall steps to set up a Wi-Fi hotspot:

Step 1 Choose a hotspot solution.

Step 2 Set up an Internet connection.

Step 3 Find and purchase equipment.

Step 4 Configure the equipment.

Step 5 Physically install the equipment.

Step 6 Test the hotspot.

This chapter explains how to complete Steps 1 and 2. After you complete the first two steps, you should continue with the chapter corresponding to the hotspot solution you choose so that you can complete the remaining steps.

Step 1: Choose a Hotspot Solution

Of course, you can research the many different hotspot solutions yourself; however, this book will save you some time by discussing four possible solutions in detail. At least one of these solutions should work well for your business or organization. If not, you can refer to the "Additional Solutions" section of this chapter, which lists more solutions; however, these solutions are not covered in detail in this book.

The following Wi-Fi hotspot solutions are described in the next few sections and also are covered in Part II, "Setting Up the Hotspot":

- Simple free access hotspot
- Advanced free access hotspot using ZoneCD
- Boingo's hotspot network to provide paid access
- Free or paid access and private network using a hotspot gateway

---

 NOTE Part II of this book walks you through the entire process of installing and setting up the four solutions for a small indoor coverage area. If you need to provide coverage for a larger area, such as a hotel, refer to Chapter 12, "Increasing Your Hotspot's Wireless Coverage," after setting up the main components.

Solution 1: Simple Free Access Hotspot

This is the simplest and least expensive of the four different solutions. The Linksys Wireless-G Broadband Router (WRT54G) used in this setup is the same type of equipment used in wireless home networks. This solution does not actually have true hotspot features, such as user control and management.

This solution is good if you do not want to require the users to log in and do not want to display a splash screen. This solution allows you to provide simple wireless Internet access to your visitors.

Solution 2: Advanced Free Access Hotspot Using ZoneCD

If you want to give away free access and desire neat hotspot features, this might be the right solution for you. You will need to dedicate a PC to this setup; however, if you have an extra PC, this solution is cost-effective. The software that does the "work" is actually free. To get the premium or advanced hotspot features, you sign up for a service plan, which ranges from $7.95 to $15.95 per month. It is free to use the basic features, though, such as the splash screen and content filtering.

Solution 3: Boingo's Hotspot Network to Provide Paid Access

Want to be part of a huge hotspot network and provide paid access? If so, this is the solution for you. Boingo, one of the biggest hotspot networks, provides service to thousands of users all over the world in airports, cafés, hotels, retail locations, and more. Setting up the equipment is fairly simple and does not require many technical skills. You actually set all this up through an off-the-self product, the Linksys Wireless-G VPN Broadband Router (WRV54G).

Solution 4: Free or Paid Access and Private Network Using a Hotspot Gateway

This solution is the most expensive option and provides an easy way to integrate or create a private network using the same Internet connection. You can provide either free or paid access with this solution. The D-Link Airspot Wireless G Public/Private Hot Spot Gateway (DSA-3200) has both public and private ports to ensure that your private and confidential information is secured from the public.

The easiest way to provide paid access with this solution is to use the Airspot Ticket Printer (DSA-3100P). You can use your existing cash register or credit card processor to take payments and then print and physically hand out the login information to your customers.

You can also set up a credit card processor for on-demand, online payments from hotspot users via the splash screen. However, this requires the use of an external RADIUS server, which is discussed in Chapter 7, "Solution 4: Free or Paid Access and Private Network Using a Hotspot Gateway."

Hotspot Features

Table 3-1 provides an overview of the features that each solution provides.

Table 3-1 *Overview of the Hotspot Solution Features*

	Solution 1: Simple	Solution 2: ZoneCD	Solution 3: Boingo	Solution 4: D-Link
Access Type	Free	Free	Paid	Free/paid
Estimated Minimum Cost	$40	$70	$160	$500
Estimated Installation Time	1 hour	3 hours	2 hours	2 hours
Hotspot Network			✔	
Roaming for Multiple Locations		✔	✔	✔
Built-In Private Ports				✔
Splash (Redirection) Screen		✔	✔	✔
Customizable Splash Screen		✔		✔
Ticketing System		✔		✔
Remote Admin Access	✔	✔	✔	✔
Content Filtering	✔	✔	✔	✔
Port Filtering	✔	✔	✔	✔
Open/Close Hours	✔	✔	✔	✔
Customizable User Time Limits		✔		✔
Bandwidth Throttling		✔		✔
Detailed Usage Reports		✔		

To give you a better idea of the hotspot features, the following list that each feature in greater detail:

- **Estimated minimum cost**—This is the minimum cost for each solution for a small hotspot that does not require extra access points.

- **Estimated installation time**—The installation times also apply only when setting up a small hotspot. This is because the time involved in installing extra access points to provide more coverage varies greatly.

- **Hotspot network**—This identifies whether the hotspot solution would be part of a large hotspot network. As you see in Table 3-1, the only solution that belongs to a hotspot network is Solution 3, where you would be a part of the Boingo Wireless network. This would allow your subscribers to access a Wi-Fi network at a different location, which could entice people to join your network. In addition, people who already have Wi-Fi service with Boingo might be attracted to your location, which improves the marketing of your company or organization.

- **Roaming for multiple locations**—This indicates that the solution somehow supports roaming or management of multiple hotspot locations.

- **Built-in private port**—This helps you easily integrate or create a private network using a single Internet connection and without the use of other equipment. The private port would securely separate the networks.

- **Splash (redirection) screen**—The splash screen provides a way to let users know of any terms and conditions of using the hotspot, the consequences of using unsecured networks, and a way to collect payment or login information before the user accesses the Internet.

- **Customizable splash screen**—This simply means you can customize the splash screen by adding things such as text and images.

- **Ticketing system**—Ticketing systems are used in conjunction with both free and fee-based hotspots. Ticketing systems enable the hotspot owners to physically hand out unique usernames and passwords to customers or visitors.

  For example, you could give out free Internet access to only paying customers. Suppose that a visitor sat down at your café, pulled out a laptop, and connected to the hotspot. The splash screen would stop the visitor from accessing the Internet. It would say that hotspot access is given only to customers, and he must get the login information from the cashier. After purchasing something, the visitor would ask for the login information. With a few clicks from the cashier, a username and password would print and be handed to the customer. The visitor would sit back down, open his laptop, access the hotspot, enter the login information, and be able to use the free Wi-Fi Internet service.

- **Remote admin access**—This feature allows you to access your hotspot's web-based configuration utility when you are away from the location. This can be handy when you are checking on your hotspot status. You can view connection logs, Internet connection status, and more anywhere via the web.

- **Content filtering**—Content filtering allows you to block specified websites or web pages containing defined keywords. The content filtering works differently for each hotspot solution.

- **Port filtering**—This allows you to block specific ports, which in turn prevents the usage of certain Internet applications.

- **Open/close hours**—This allows you to specify the times you would like your hotspot to be active. For example, you might not want to have the hotspot on while your business is closed.

- **Customizable user time limits**—Applying time limits to users can be useful, especially when you are providing free access. For example, you can limit each user to one hour of access per day or over a specified amount of time.

- **Bandwidth throttling**—With this feature, you can control the amount of bandwidth that is available to users. You could set an upload and download throttle limit.

- **Detailed usage reports**—Usage reports tell you how much your hotspot is being used, when it is being used, and how it is being used. This can let you know some important information about your hotspot users.

Sam's Coffee Shop—Choosing a Hotspot Solution

In the previous chapter, Sam went through the business-related benefits and costs of hosting a hotspot in his coffee shop. He decided he wanted to provide free access to his hotspot; however, he did not know which solution would be best for his situation. After reading Chapter 2, though, he is certain that Solution 2—using the ZoneCD—would be best. He did not pick Solution 1 because it does not provide the splash screen and other hotspot features he wants to have. He thought Solution 4, using the D-Link hotspot gateway, was a bit too expensive for his budget.

To save some money on his hotspot solution, Sam is thinking about using an old family computer with the ZoneCD software. Just in case he decides not to dedicate the PC for this purpose, he spoke to a local electronics shop, which said he could get a simple computer fairly cheap that would work with the ZoneCD.

For the first month, the plan is to sign up for one of the premium services provided by ZoneCD so that Sam can see how all the features work. If it looks like the features are being put to use, he will keep the service; however, he thinks the free version will be adequate for his situation.

Additional Solutions

If you are looking for specific features and functionalities in your hotspot solution and they are not supported in the four solutions discussed in detail in this book, do not worry; many other solutions exist.

Even though this book does not step you through the installation and setup of these additional solutions, you can still benefit from this book.

Following are several other solutions that you should consider implementing:

- Use low-cost wireless routers with replacement firmware.

  You can use a Linksys Wireless Router (WRT-54GL or other support models and brands) that is loaded with open source firmware, such as DD-WRT or Sveasoft. These replacement firmwares give you many neat and usually expensive features, such as a splash screen (also known as *captive portal*), multiple service set identifiers (SSID), VLANs, and repeater mode, all at no or low additional cost.

  For easy remote administration, better usage reports, the ability to accept payments, or when deploying and managing multiple hotspot locations, you can use a service such as SputnikNet with a supported wireless router and the DD-WRT replacement firmware.

  For more information about DD-WRT replacement firmware, visit http://www.dd-wrt.com.

  For more information about Sveasoft, visit http://www.sveasoft.com.

  For more information about SputnikNet service, visit http://www.sputnik.com.

- Use low-cost wireless routers and software on a PC.

  Similar to ZoneCD, which is one of four step-by-step solutions in this book, the following software titles act as the wireless controller, or hotspot gateway, used in conjunction with a basic wireless router, such as the Linksys WRT-54GL:

  - **Less Networks's Hotspot Server**—For more information, visit http://www.lessnetworks.com.

  - **PatronSoft's FirstSpot Windows-based Wi-Fi hotspot management software**—For more information, visit http://www.patronsoft.com.

  - **Antamedia's HotSpot Software**—For more information, visit http://www.antamedia.com.

- Use a hotspot gateway.

  Using hotspot gateways is more expensive than the other methods; however, this method also offers advantages, such as the ability to use hotspot ticket printers. In addition, hotspot gateways provide a more plug-and-play installation and are typically better suited for enterprise-type environments.

  The following are hotspot gateways, other than the D-Link solution that is discussed in detail in this book, that you might want to use for your hotspot:

  — Versa's 802.11b/g Multifunction Hot Spot Subscriber/Gateway (Model #VX-HG11G) with optional ticket printer

    The gateway has separate public and private Ethernet ports, allowing easy integration of your public and private networks.

    For more information, visit http://www.versatek.com.

  — SMC's EliteConnect Wireless Hotspot Gateway (model #SMCWHSG44-G) with optional ticket printer

    Multiple WAN ports can pump up to four Internet connections into your network to create a super-fast hotspot or to guarantee an always-on connection.

    For more information, visit http://www.smc.com.

  — Airepoch's 802.11 b/G High-Speed Feature-Rich Indoor HotSpot Access Gateway with optional ticket printer

    This also has multiple WAN ports that can pump two Internet connections into your network to create a fast hotspot or to guarantee an always-on connection.

    For more information, visit http://www.echotechwireless.com.

  — ZyXEL's 802.11g Wireless Hot Spot Gateway (model #G-4100R) with optional ticket printer

    This gateway provides outgoing Simple Mail Transfer Protocol (SMTP) server redirection to help control and eliminate spam from your hotspot.

    For more information, visit http://www.zyxel.com.

Typically, to remotely manage your hotspot(s), to view better usage reports, to accept online payments, or when deploying and managing multiple hotspot locations, you should use a hotspot billing service. Following are a few companies that offer these types of RADIUS service:

- **WirelessOrbit**—http://www.wirelessorbit.com/
- **ALEPPOE**—http://www.alepo.com/
- **Pronto Networks**—http://www.prontonetworks.com

 NOTE A convenient list of the websites mentioned in this section is available at the companion website:

http://www.wifihotspotbook.com/bonus_materials/

Step 2: Set Up an Internet Connection

You might already have an Internet connection established in your home. That is not much different from the Internet connection you could have for your hotspot. Whether or not you have experience with various Internet connections, you need to pay a little more attention to the features and choose a type of connection that will satisfy the needs of your hotspot users.

Choosing the Right Internet Connect Type

Internet connections are of many different types. Table 3-2 shows several that you can use with your hotspot.

Table 3-2 *Overview of Internet Connections*

Type	Download Speed	Upload Speed	Suggested Hotspot Size	Start-Up Cost	Monthly Cost
ADSL	1500–8000 kbps	64–640 kbps	Small	$0–$100	$35–$100
SDSL	128–1500 kbps	128–1500 kbps	Small/medium	$0–$300	$80–$300
Fixed wireless broadband	768–2000 kbps	256–2000 kbps	Small/medium	$0–$300	$80–$200
Cable	400–4000 kbps	128–4000 kbps	Small/medium	$0–$100	$60–$150
T1	384–1500 kbps	384–1500 kbps	Large	$500–$2000	$300–$2000
Satellite	600 kbps	128 kbps	Small	$800–$1000	$125–$300

The download and upload speeds are approximate speeds that the particular Internet connections should operate within. The exact speeds, however, differ depending on the Internet service provider (ISP).

When looking for Internet service for your hotspot, keep in mind that the bigger your hotspot is, the bigger and better your Internet connection should be. This is because you will likely have more users actively using the Internet simultaneously with a larger hotspot; thus, you need to be able to support these users with reasonable speeds. Table 3-2 shows hotspot sizes that should work well with each Internet connection type, and Table 3-3 defines the hotspot sizes.

Table 3-3   *Defining the Recommend Hotspot Sizes*

Suggested Hotspot Size	Estimated Number of Simultaneous Users
Small	1–10
Medium	11–20
Large	21–50

Evaluating the hotspot size and figuring out the necessary Internet connection usually depends on the number of concurrent, or simultaneous, users. Of course, you do not know exactly how many users your hotspot will receive and when; however, you should be able to estimate a range, such as those defined in Table 3-3.

The start-up costs include the fees for equipment, such as a modem, and installation services necessary to get your Internet connection up and going. Monthly costs are what you should expect to pay on a continual basis.

"Always-On" Internet Connections

Broadband Internet services, such as digital subscriber line (DSL), cable, and T1 lines, provide an "always-on" connection. Unlike dialup service, the modems for these connections do not need to dial a phone number; you do not have to wait and listen for the connection to be established. You are always connected to the Internet when you need it.

DSL Internet Connections

When looking at DSL Internet service, keep in mind that several versions exist. The most common is Asymmetric DSL (ADSL), which is often found in homes and small businesses. Its bandwidth is devoted mostly to the downstream, giving much faster download speeds than upload speeds. However, the upstream speeds provided are usually adequate for small businesses and hotspot applications. For example, when you are downloading music files, watching a video stream, and browsing websites, the data is moving mostly downstream from the Internet to your computer.

Symmetric DSL (SDSL) is commonly found in small- or medium-sized businesses. This connection can provide the same amount of bandwidth for the up and down streams, thus allowing a much greater upload rate than ADSL. This is beneficial if your Wi-Fi hotspot users need to send e-mails with large attachments.

The quality of DSL service you experience is usually related to how close your location is to the telecom facility. Therefore, not all areas have DSL service, especially in rural areas, or you might get DSL service, but the performance might not be very good.

Fixed Wireless Broadband

Companies called wireless Internet service providers (WISPs) deliver Internet connections to homes and businesses via radio waves instead of physical lines. Therefore, fixed wireless broadband Internet access is typically located where DSL or cable Internet service is absent. WISPs typically use high mounting places—such as cell phone, radio, and cell towers—for their radios to achieve a widespread coverage area.

The quality and speeds of these Internet connections vary greatly depending on the location of your facility within the WISP coverage area.

Cable Internet Connections

Cable Internet is generally available in residential areas, but you should still check the accessibility at your location. Unlike other Internet services, cable connections are shared among users in your area. Therefore, the speeds you experience will vary, depending on the overall usage at that moment. However, cable Internet connections generally provide overall better performance than DSL. If you have a choice, go with a cable connection.

T1 Internet Connections

T1 lines are dedicated Internet connections commonly found only in large businesses where guaranteed bandwidth, or speed, is required. T1 lines offer good, reliable performance, but they are expensive. A more affordable solution is to lease a fractional T1 line. Large hotspots that need to support loads of concurrent users, such as in larger hotels, should have a T1 line or similar fast and high-quality Internet connection.

Satellite

If your facility is in the "digital darkness," or in a place devoid of high-speed Internet services, you are most likely a candidate for satellite Internet service.

Satellite Internet service is available in most places; however, because of the delay of the signals transmitting such far distances, certain applications, such as voice over IP (VoIP) or virtual private networks (VPNs), might not work well. Satellite Internet service also usually requires a one- or two-year contract, and it is typically more expensive than the other options, which might be a roadblock.

Questions to Ask ISPs

When searching for an ISP, ask many questions, such as these:

- **What package discounts are being offered?**—The majority of telecom service providers, such as telephone, cellular, and cable companies, offer package discounts when you sign up for multiple services. Keep this in mind when you are looking for your Internet service. For example, some cable companies offer Internet and digital phone service along with their regular services.

- **Will you have to sign a contract?**—Be careful, because some ISPs require you to sign a one- or two-year contract when signing up for Internet service. It is a good idea to look into any money-back guarantees that these ISPs might offer before signing a contract.

- **Will you receive a static or dynamic IP address?**—Residential-class Internet services typically provide you with only a dynamic IP address, which changes periodically. However, most business-class ISPs give you the option of a static IP address. This helps if you will remotely connect, via the Internet, to your hotspot, or network, when you are away from the actual hotspot location.

 NOTE   Your Internet IP address is a series of numbers (such as 66.249.64.14) that identifies and points to your specific Internet connection at your location. IP addresses can easily be logged when visiting websites. This helps identify people who commit fraud and other illegal activities on the Internet.

TIP If you have a dynamic IP address (which changes frequently), you can use a service such as Dynamic DNS through DynDNS, which gives you a domain name (such as yourname.getmyip.net) to use instead of your Internet IP address. This domain name automatically points to the current IP address of your Internet connection or network. You can sign up for the service at http://www.dyndns.com and then make any required changes on your network.

Linksys wireless routers typically have a special section in their web-based configuration screens to input your DynDNS account information.

- **Will you receive free dialup Internet access?**—Many ISPs offer complimentary dialup Internet access to their high-speed Internet customers so that they can have an Internet connection while they are away from their main location. This can come in handy while traveling if your hotel does not have free Internet access available. In addition, you can use the dialup access during outages of your main Internet connection.

- **How many e-mail addresses will you receive?**—Most ISPs provide you with POP3 e-mail accounts. This can be useful if you do not have a good e-mail account already. Some ISPs also provide a web-based e-mail system; that way, you can easily view your e-mail through a web browser, rather than using a client software program.

NOTE POP3 e-mail accounts are different from other e-mail systems used by some ISPs, such as America Online (AOL). When you get a POP3 account, you are given mail server addresses, a username, a password, and other information. You can then input this information into e-mail client programs, such as Microsoft Outlook. After you set up the system, you typically press a button to synchronize, or send and receive, your e-mail. The addressing methods, though, are the same as with other e-mail services. For instance, you will still get an e-mail address similar to yourname@website.com when using a POP3 e-mail account.

- **Will you receive website space?**—Various ISPs might furnish you with web space for your own website. If your business or organization does not already have a presence on the web, this can be useful. Some ISPs give you a virtual domain name, such as yourname.yourisp.com. On the other hand, some even pay for a domain name registration so that you can get your own domain, such as yourname.com.

Sam's Coffee Shop—Choosing an Internet Connection

Now Sam needs to decide which Internet connection would be best for his situation. He does not think his hotspot will receive many simultaneous users, so he does not think he needs a high-quality Internet connection. He thinks that the ADSL or cable Internet connections would work fine.

After visiting some websites, he finds a few possible scenarios with local companies:

Table 3-4

Type	Download Speed	Upload Speed	E-Mail Accounts	Free Dialup	Start-Up Cost	Monthly Cost
ADSL	1.5–3.0 Mbps	384–12 kbps	11	Yes	$13	$54.99
Cable	768 kbps	128 kbps	5	No	Free	$69.95

He decides to go with the DSL small-business-class service because it will provide greater speeds, has free dialup access, and costs less than the cable option overall. The only thing Sam does not like is that he has to pay the shipping for the self-installation kit and must install the DSL equipment himself. The cable provider performs a free installation, whereas the DSL company charges $300 for a professional installation.

Usage/Legal Terms of Provider

Make sure that the Internet service you choose allows you to set up a hotspot and share the Internet connection with others. For instance, in homes it is usually illegal to let others outside your home use your network, even when you are not charging them for use. Most business-class Internet services do allow you to share the Internet connection; however, double-check to make sure you are good to go. You certainly want to avoid legal issues and heavy fines!

Getting the Internet Connection

If do not already have an Internet connection at your location that you will try to share or use for your hotspot, you need to set one up. Many ISPs are available. To start the search, you could check with your local cable and telephone providers, because they likely offer some type of Internet service plan. They will either schedule an appointment to come out and do the installation, or they will provide a self-installation kit.

NOTE   You can refer to the following website when searching for a WISP:

http://www.bbwexchange.com/wisps/

Following are a few websites of satellite Internet providers that you might want to check out:

http://www.hughesnetbiz.com
http://www.starband.com
http://www.skycasters.com

A convenient list of these websites is available at the companion website:

http://www.wifihotspotbook.com/bonus_materials/

Where to Install the Connection

Make sure the Internet connection device, or modem, is installed where you want to put the wireless router or hotspot gateway. During the installation, you have to physically connect these two pieces of equipment. Remember, it is best to put these components as close as possible to the intended coverage area. In some cases, such as in installations for larger hotspots that require more than one access point, you might install this equipment in a back office or utility closet.

NOTE   If you are installing a larger hotspot, you might want to refer to Chapter 12 before deciding where to install the Internet connection. This will help you better understand how these larger hotspots are set up and where it is ideal to place the Internet modem with each type of approach.

You will probably be limited to where you can hook up the modem, because it will connect to a cable outlet for cable Internet or to a telephone jack when using a DSL Internet connection. If these outlets are not in a good spot, you can have your cable or phone company install a more convenient outlet. The installation of a new outlet will probably cost you $100 or more, however.

Chapter Review

As stated in this chapter, the main steps of starting a Wi-Fi hotspot are as follows:

Step 1 Choose a hotspot solution.

Step 2 Set up an Internet connection.

Step 3 Find and purchase equipment.

Step 4 Configure the equipment.

Step 5 Physically install the equipment.

Step 6 Test the hotspot.

After reading this chapter, you should know what hotspot solution you want to deploy and what Internet connection you will be using. Therefore, you can mark Steps 1 and 2 as done.

If you choose one of the four hotspot solutions covered in detail, you can continue with the applicable chapter in Part II of this book to complete the remaining steps. Otherwise, follow the vendor or manufacturer installation and setup instructions, keeping in mind that you can still refer to other chapters, such as in Part III, "After Your Wi-Fi Hotspot Is Alive," during the installation and administration of your hotspot.

Part II: **Setting Up the Hotspot**

Chapter 4   Solution 1: Simple Free Access Hotspot

Chapter 5   Solution 2: Advanced Free Access Hotspot Using ZoneCD

Chapter 6   Solution 3: Join Boingo's Hotspot Network to Provide
Paid Access

Chapter 7   Solution 4: Free or Paid Access and Private Network
Using a Hotspot Gateway

Chapter 4

Solution 1:
Simple Free Access Hotspot

As mentioned earlier in the book, a free access hotspot solution is simple and inexpensive, but it does not provide any real "hotspot features," such as user control and management. However, some organizations, like yours, might not need these features. Your business might simply want to provide the public with wireless Internet access without the thrills. By offering a free hotspot, you might attract more customers.

The simple free hotspot solution, as seen in Figure 4-1, is set up just like any other simple wireless network, such as those in homes. A wireless router connects to the Internet via an Internet modem.

Figure 4-1   Solution Network Layout Diagram

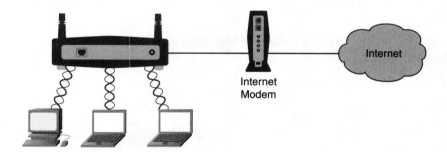

The hotspot users wirelessly connect to the wireless router. They are not prompted with a splash or redirection screen with this solution; therefore, the hotspot users have uncontrolled access to the Internet. Most wireless routers, however, let you set some restrictions and filters to help control users, but these functions are not as extensive as those offered by a "real hotspot gateway."

The overall steps to complete when setting up a simple free access solution are as follows:

Step 1   Gather the necessary items.

Step 2   Set up the wireless router.

Step 3   Configure additional settings.

The following sections will help you through each step.

Step 1: Gather the Necessary Items

The hardware for the simple free hotspot solution consists of a wireless router.

When looking for the equipment, it is best to stick with the recommended products. These products are used in this book when showing applicable configuration screens, so if you are new to wireless, it is highly recommended that you use this same equipment.

TIP Most of the equipment that you need for the simple free hotspot should be available at local consumer electronics stores. You might also try searching Internet stores, such as Amazon.com and Buy.com.

No specific features are required for the wireless router; it just needs to be compliant with Wi-Fi.

Figure 4-2 shows the Linksys Wireless-G Broadband Router, which is the wireless router I recommend.

Figure 4-2   Recommended Wireless Router

The Linksys Wireless-G Broadband Router (model #WRT54G) typically costs between $25 and $70, depending on where you purchase it.

Step 2: Set Up the Wireless Router

To set up your wireless router, follow the manufacturer instructions that are included with the product. Some vendors might have written guides, and some might want you to use a CD that will help with the wireless router setup. The installation instructions will most likely have you configure some initial settings, but you will need to keep in mind several things, as discussed in the following list. Do not worry if you are not prompted during the setup to configure all these items, because you will have a chance to change all the settings later.

- Do not use security or encryption methods.
- Use a service set identifier (SSID—network name) that describes your business/ organization or attentions. For example, a café might use "Free Hotspot at Bob's Café." If the hotspot is being put in just for the local youth club, you might want to use something such as "Youth Club Hotspot."
- Configure a channel that is not being used by other nearby wireless networks. You should also try to use the nonoverlapping channels of 1, 6, and 11. However, try to avoid channel 6, because it is the default channel that most wireless devices use; therefore, it is likely the most congested channel.
- Use mixed mode so that users who have either B or G wireless adapters can connect to your hotspot.

Step 3: Configure Additional Settings

We will go through some additional settings that are useful in public hotspot solutions, which you probably were not prompted for during the initial setup. You might need to refer to your wireless router documentation for specific instructions on some of the settings, because all wireless routers work differently.

The following sections go into more detail on these additional settings.

Accessing the Web-Based Configuration Utility

Most wireless routers have a small built-in web server inside the box that enables you to easily access a web-based configuration utility (see Figure 4-3 for an example) to change settings. After connecting to the wireless router, you usually bring up your web browser (such as Internet Explorer) and enter the IP address of the wireless router. For example, 192.168.1.1, 192.168.0.1, and 192.168.2.1 are common default IP addresses for wireless routers. Your wireless router user guide will explain which IP address to use. You then are prompted to log in. Again, the user guide tells you what username and password to use when logging into the router for the first time. After logging into the router, you should see a configuration utility screen similar to Figure 4-3.

NOTE Change the default password for your wireless router configuration utility. Most setup wizards prompt you to do so; however, make sure you do it yourself to prevent unauthorized access to the utility.

Figure 4-3   Example of a Web-Based Configuration Utility

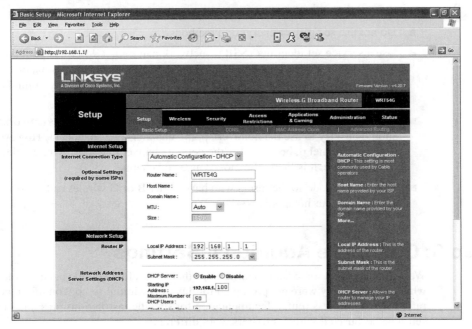

DHCP User Limit

Most wireless routers let you specify how many IP addresses to hand out through DHCP. Limiting the number of DHCP users basically limits how many users can connect to the wireless network, or hotspot, at once.

For example, suppose a hotspot owner wants to limit the number of concurrent users to 10, because he has only a basic DSL Internet connection, and he does not think it is fast enough to support many more than 10 users. Therefore, he limits the number of DHCP users to 10.

You can usually find the DHCP settings in the basic settings section of your configuration utility or in a section named DHCP. Some wireless routers have a specific entry for the maximum number of DHCP users, as shown in Figure 4-4. Other wireless routers might not have such a clear way of setting this feature, but you can usually change the ending IP address to indicate how many IP addresses you want to give out, based on the starting IP address. For example, if the starting IP address is 192.168.0.100 and you set the ending IP address to 192.168.0.109, you will be limiting access to nine DHCP users.

Figure 4-4 DHCP User Limit

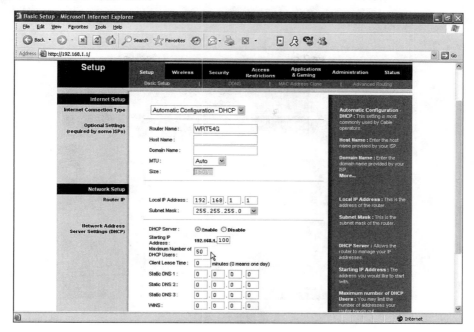

AP Isolation

AP isolation, also known as Publicly Secure Packet Forwarding (PSPF), is less common than other features found in wireless routers. When enabled, it isolates each user from the other users. This gives some extra security to the hotspot users by preventing people from accessing shared files of other users.

You usually find this feature in the Advanced Wireless settings, and you usually can simply turn it on and off, as shown in Figure 4-5.

Figure 4-5   Example of the AP Isolation Setting

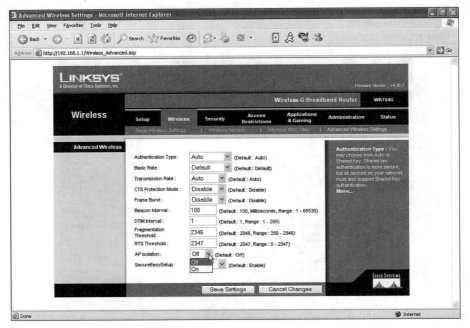

VPN Passthrough

This feature allows virtual private network (VPN) connections to pass through the wireless router. This feature should automatically be enabled by default, and you should have no reason to disable it. VPN connections allow users to securely connect to remote corporate networks via the Internet. They are also useful on hotspots to encrypt the user data that is passing through the public hotspot. Just to make sure, you should double-check that this feature is enabled on your wireless router. You might find this feature in the Misc. or Security section of the configuration utility, as shown in Figure 4-6.

Figure 4-6   Example of the VPN Passthrough Setting

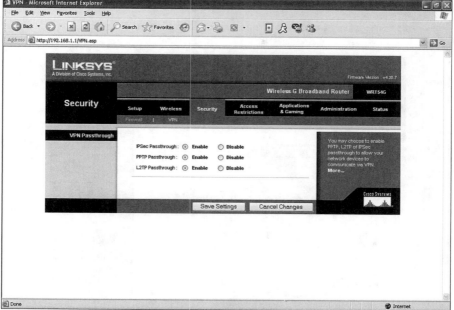

Access Restrictions

Most wireless routers enable you to specify the days or times that you want Internet access to be available. Suppose that you want people to use the hotspot only during normal business hours. You can easily set up the wireless router to offer Internet access only Monday through Friday. Then, if the wireless router supports it, you can set it to be available only from 9 a.m. to 5 p.m. during those days.

You might find this feature in the Access Restrictions section, as shown in Figure 4-7, or with the filter settings of your wireless router admin utility.

Figure 4-7   Example of the Access Restrictions Setting

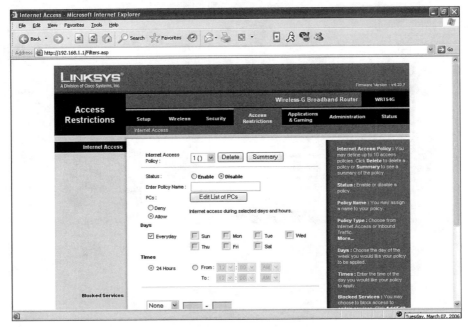

Blocked Services

Wireless routers allow you to block certain services—such as FTP, POP3, and Simple
Mail Transfer Protocol (SMTP)—from passing through the router. You can do this by
blocking the ports used by the application you want to prevent, such as ports 20 and 21
for FTP, port 110 for POP3, and port 25 for SMTP. You also might want to block certain
services to prevent illegal activities, such as spamming, or the usage of certain file-
sharing programs.

You might find this feature in the Access Restrictions section, as shown in Figure 4-8,
or with the filter settings of your wireless router admin utility. All wireless routers
differ in the way you set this up, however. If possible, block all ports (services) except
for a few, just to be on the safe side. You might be able to edit a list of approved ports,
rather than making a long list of ports to block. Allowing only the following ports
might work in your situation:

- 80 for web browsing (HTTP)
- 443 for secure web browsing (HTTPS)
- 110 for e-mail retrieval (POP3)

Figure 4-8   Example of the Blocked Services Setting

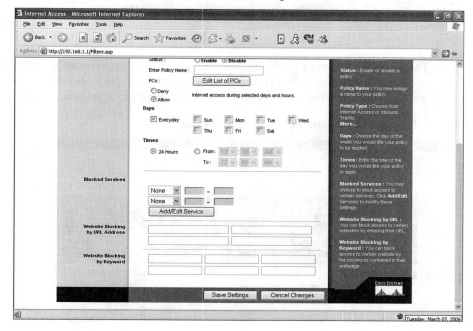

Remote Router Access

Your wireless router should support remote access or management. This lets you easily access the configuration utility via the Internet to check the status and change settings when you are away from the hotspot.

You can usually find this feature within the Administration section of your wireless router configuration utility, as shown in Figure 4-9. By default, this feature is disabled. If you have the option to use SSL access (HTTPS), you should. In addition, to provide more security, some wireless routers might allow you to give remote access capability to only a certain IP address.

For example, if you know that you will access the hotspot configuration utility only from home, you could input the IP address of your home Internet connection.

NOTE   Make sure that when you reference an IP address, it is a static IP address. If you have a dynamic IP address (which changes frequently), you can use a service such as Dynamic DNS to obtain a domain name (such as yourname.getmyip.net) to use instead of your Internet IP address. This domain name will automatically point to the current IP address of your Internet connection or network. You can sign up for the service at http://www.dyndns.com. Then make any required changes on your network.

Linksys wireless routers have a special section in their web-based configuration screens where you can input your DynDNS account information.

Then, only people from your home network would be able to remotely access the hotspot configuration utility. However, this feature is not crucial because someone would also need to know your wireless router password to access the utility.

Figure 4-9   Example of the Remote Router Access Setting

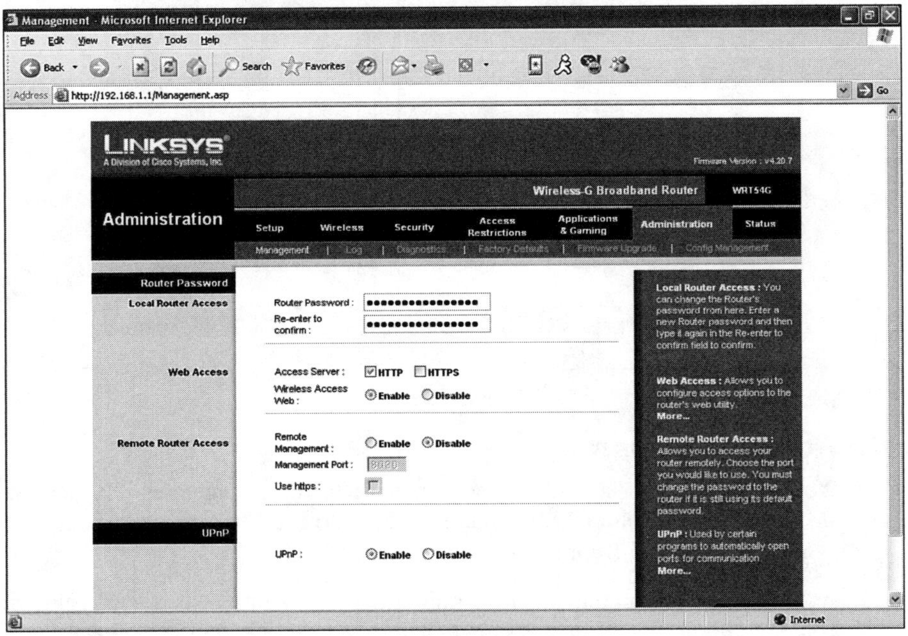

Web-Based Configuration Utility Access Server

Some wireless routers allow you to choose which type of server you use to access the web-based configuration utility. If you can, use an HTTPS (SSL) server. SSL encrypts the data between your computer and the internal web server of the wireless router. If you do not use SSL and you log into the configuration utility the default way (HTTP), anyone who is using the right tools can retrieve your wireless router password when you log in.

As Figure 4-10 shows, this feature might be in the Administration section of your wireless router configuration utility.

Figure 4-10   Example of the Web-Based Configuration Utility Access Server Setting

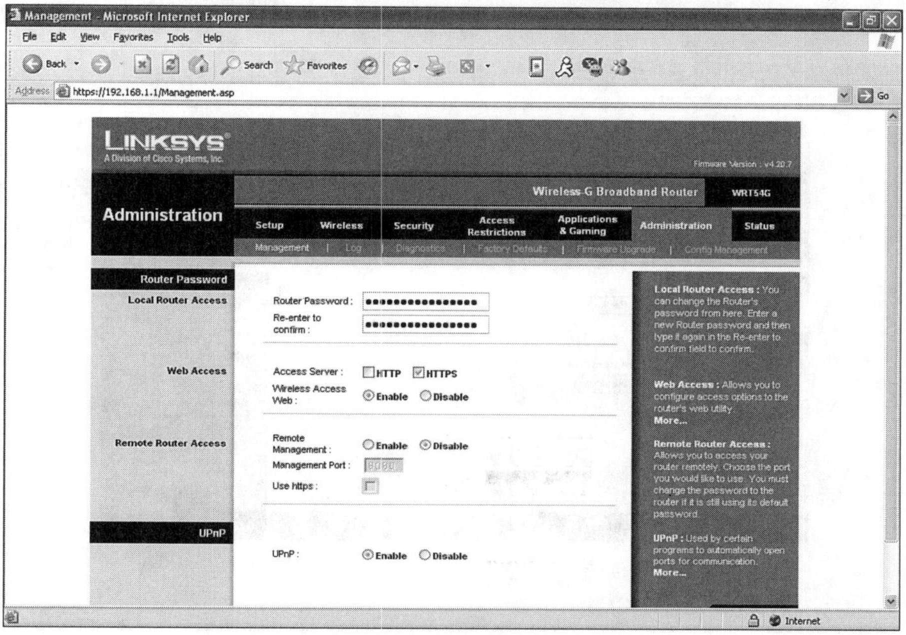

Backup Configuration

After spending all this time configuring your wireless router, save the configuration. Then, if you have problems later and need to do a hard reset, it will take less time. You could just point to the backup file and load the saved settings, rather than reconfiguring all of them.

This feature will likely be in the Administration section, as shown in Figure 4-11, or the Tools section of your wireless router configuration utility.

Figure 4-11   Example of the Backup Configuration Setting

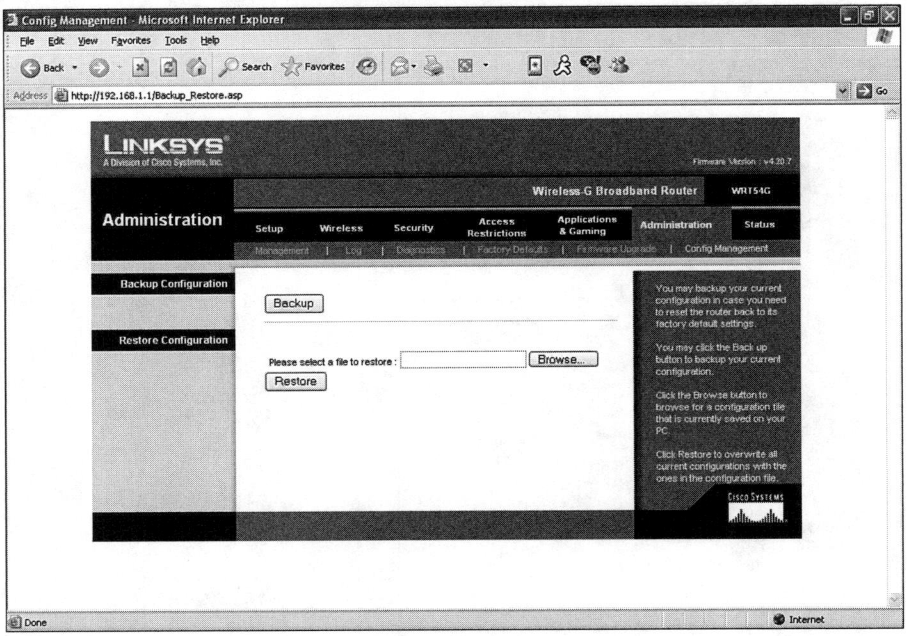

Congratulations! You are finished!

Chapter Review

Solution 1 does not provide real "hotspot features," such as user control and management, and web page redirection or splash screens; however, this solution is inexpensive and might work when only simple Internet access is required.

Keep in mind the following:

- Use the particular wireless router that is recommended in this chapter.
- Refer to the tips and recommendations when setting up your wireless router.

Chapter 5

Solution 2: Advanced Free Access Hotspot Using ZoneCD

Public IP, the creator of ZoneCD, gives hotspot operators a simple, highly versatile, free, open source Wi-Fi hotspot solution. All levels of free Wi-Fi providers, from experienced programmers to coffee shop owners, can use ZoneCD. Setting up a free Wi-Fi hotspot can be as easy as hooking up an access point, popping in a CD, and rebooting a computer.

The ZoneCD software is known as a LiveCD. The software does not install on your hard drive; it runs right from your CD-ROM. The software is what controls the hotspot access and provides all the hotspot features. ZoneCD is basically a mini operating system that starts when the CD is in the CD-ROM drive during the booting process of your computer. The software automatically detects the computer hardware and supports many graphics cards, sound cards, and other peripherals.

NOTE   Secure Shell (SSH) provides a secure way to access remote computers.

ZoneCD is in a Linux operating system format, but you do not have to know anything about Linux to use ZoneCD. You just need to know how to place a CD in a CD-ROM drive, turn on a computer, and go through the setup screens. This provides all the benefits of Linux, such as stability, configurability, and security, without your having to do anything with Linux. Keep in mind that you must dedicate a computer to run ZoneCD. You will not be able to use this computer for anything else. You can, however, use an older computer, because ZoneCD operating requirements are relatively low.

ZoneCD was designed for easy and secure connection to an existing private network. However, you do not have to have a private network to use ZoneCD.

The ZoneCD solution, as depicted in Figure 5-1, works by adding a PC (running the ZoneCD software) between an access point, or wireless router, which provides the public wireless access, and your private network (or Internet connection). You are not restricted in terms of which access point or wireless router you must use to provide the public access; the access point or router just needs to be Wi-Fi-compliant. The same is true of your private network router. It just needs to be a standard router.

If you want to put the computer between two network devices, as described, the computer must have two Ethernet network interface cards installed (depicted as Eth0 and Eth1 in Figure 5-1). A firewall is formed at ZoneCD, which protects the optional private network from public access.

Figure 5-1   ZoneCD Network Layout Diagram

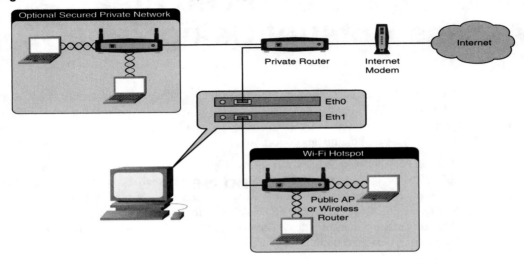

As shown in Figure 5-1, hotspot users wirelessly connect to an access point or wireless router, which is physically connected to the computer that is running the ZoneCD software. When the hotspot user tries to access the Internet, the ZoneCD solution intervenes and might require him to register or log in, or it might redirect him to a web page before he can freely browse the web.

If you apply usage limits, the ZoneCD solution enforces them and takes action when needed. For example, you might limit users to one hour of hotspot use per day. The ZoneCD system keeps track of usage times and notifies a user before he reaches his time limit. When the user reaches the time limit, ZoneCD cuts off his Internet access.

NOTE   If you have specific questions on how the ZoneCD solution works, you can visit the Public IP website at http://www.publicip.net or http://www.publicip.com.

The overall steps to complete when setting up the ZoneCD solution are as follows:

Step 1 Choose the mode and service.

Step 2 Gather the necessary items.

Step 3 Set up and configure the access points and routers.

Step 4 Perform a physical installation.

Step 5 Perform ZoneCD initial setup.

The following sections guide you through each step.

Step 1: Choose the Mode and Service

ZoneCD can operate in two modes, which you designate later, during the initial setup:

- Open
- Closed

 NOTE The Open mode can always be used free of charge. When using Closed mode, you have the choice to use the free features (as discussed in this section) or purchase Public IP premium services (discussed in the section "Services Overview") for even more features.

Open Mode

If you choose to run ZoneCD in Open mode, users are shown a simple splash page, as shown in Figure 5-2, the first time they access the Internet, and then they are allowed to freely browse the web. This mode gives your hotspot only basic features, such as these:

- Home page redirection
- ZoneCD splash screen
- Content filtering (blocks inappropriate material)
- Ability to customize firewall rules (protect your private network)

Figure 5-2   Open Mode Splash Screen Example

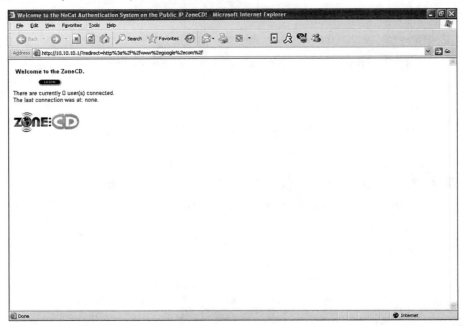

Running ZoneCD in Open mode is a good method to use if you are not concerned about keeping track of the number of users per day or requiring the user to log in to use the hotspot.

Closed Mode

If you choose to run ZoneCD in Closed mode, you bring the full power of the remotely located Zone Control server into play. This mode provides many more features than Open mode does. Just like Open mode, in Closed mode users are shown a splash screen the first time they access the Internet; however, in Closed mode, users see the splash screen customized with your logo and name, as shown in Figure 5-3.

Figure 5-3   Closed Mode Splash Screen Example for the Free Service

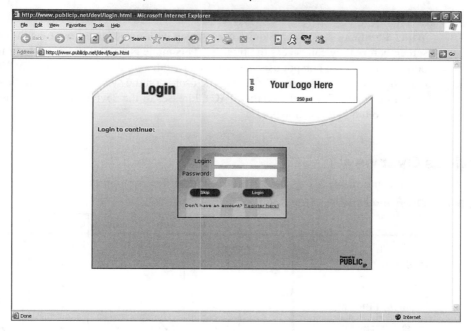

The features (available for free) that are provided in Closed mode are as follows:

- Home page redirection
- Customizable ZoneCD splash screen
- Content filtering (blocks inappropriate material)
- Customizable firewall rules (protect your private network)
- User authentication/registration
- Bandwidth throttling
- Daily time limits
- Daily download limits
- Zone open and closed times
- Blocking by MAC address
- Configuration of end-user network permissions (classes)
- Daily log e-mailer program
- Branded "Terms of Use" template, or use of your own
- Usage statistics

- Multilingual user login pages
- End-user reporting

With Closed mode, you can require users to log in or create an account via the splash screen before they can access the Internet. This mode is good if you want to limit the performance of the hotspot user, such as bandwidth and allowed IP ports. The Zone Control server keeps track of how long the user is on the system, the total uplink and downlink bandwidth used, and the MAC addresses of the device that the user used to connect to the wireless hotspot.

Services Overview

As shown in Table 5-1, Public IP offers many different services.

Table 5-1 *Overview of the Hotspot Solution Features*

	FreeNet	FreeNet	Basic	Custom	On Spot	Premium
Mode	Open	Closed	Closed	Closed	Closed	Closed
Monthly Cost	—	—	$7.95	$10.95	$12.95	$15.95
Splash Screen	✓	✓	✓	✓	✓	✓
Content Filtering	✓	✓	✓	✓	✓	✓
User Classes		✓	✓	✓	✓	✓
Bandwidth Throttling		✓	✓	✓	✓	✓
Usage Limits		✓	✓	✓	✓	✓
Open/Close Hours		✓	✓	✓	✓	✓
Walled Garden		✓	✓	✓	✓	✓
Unauthenticated Access		✓	✓	✓	✓	✓
Firewall	✓	✓	✓	✓	✓	✓
Usage Report		✓	✓	✓	✓	✓
Blocked User Report			✓	✓	✓	✓
Content Filter Report			✓	✓	✓	✓
Block P2P Software			✓	✓	✓	✓
Registration Filters			✓	✓	✓	✓
Configure DHCP			✓	✓	✓	✓
Remote Restart/Reboot			✓	✓	✓	✓
Content Filter Interface			✓	✓	✓	✓
Ticket System			✓	✓	✓	✓

Table 5-1   *Overview of the Hotspot Solution Features (Continued)*

	FreeNet	FreeNet	Basic	Custom	On Spot	Premium
Availability Hours			✓	✓	✓	✓
Spot Check			✓	✓	✓	✓
High Availability			✓	✓	✓	✓
Custom Support E-Mails			✓	✓	✓	✓
Hotspot Directory			✓	✓	✓	✓
End-User FAQ			✓	✓	✓	✓
Templates			✓	✓	✓	✓
Change Eth1 IP			✓	✓	✓	✓
Add LAN Printer			✓	✓	✓	✓
Use Remote Proxy			✓	✓	✓	✓
Remote SMTP			✓	✓	✓	✓
Configuration Queue			✓	✓	✓	✓
Encrypted Downloads			✓	✓	✓	✓
Live End-User Support					✓	✓
Customize Templates				✓		✓

The following sections describe the hotspot features so that you can get a better idea of what they offer.

Splash Screen

The splash screen template can be branded with your company or organization logo (except in Open mode). The splash pages are available in Dutch, French, German, Spanish, and English. Figure 5-4 shows an example of a splash screen for hotspots using the premium services.

Figure 5-4   Closed Mode Splash Screen Example for the Premium Services

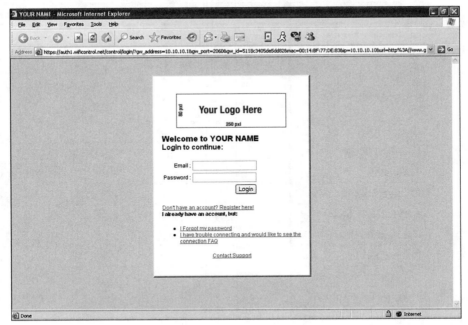

Content Filtering

ZoneCD runs an unmodified version of Dansguardian, an open source content filter. Dansguardian is configurable inside Zone Control and is based on the user classes. The content filter configuration is downloaded to your ZoneCD system during boot or using the queue system. This feature is useful and is recommended for places such as libraries, schools, youth clubs, and any other organization that wants to block inappropriate content, such as foul language and pornography.

User Classes

ZoneCD uses a user class system to assign special rights and privileges to users. All users in your zone, or hotspot, are members of a class or group. Four user classes exist:

- Protected
- Liberated
- Trusted
- Super

You can assign each user class a predefined limit for bandwidth, data transfer, and usage time. Protected or Liberated classes can be configured to use the content filter. The Protected user class default firewall rule is to block your defined open ports. The Liberated user class default firewall rule is to allow (you define ports to block). Trusted and Super user classes have no firewall rules; only (optional) time and transfer limits are applied to users in these classes. Super users are given special access to LAN resources. To determine new user classes, you define a default user class for new users to be added upon registration.

The user class feature is useful in any organization in which you want to provide certain privileges to different hotspot users. For example, you can assign the Super class to yourself and all your staff members so that you do not have limitations, such as speed, content, and private network access, while using the hotspot.

Bandwidth Throttling

You can control the amount of bandwidth available to a user in each user class by setting the upload and download speeds for each user class. This comes in handy if you will share a single Internet connection between a private network and a public hotspot. You can limit the upload and download speeds that hotspot users receive so that they do not take up all the bandwidth or speed of the Internet connection. This allows users on the private network to have the performance they need.

Time and Transfer Limits

You can configure data and time limits on a daily, weekly, or monthly basis. You can define usage limits by user class or for individual users. Temporary limits can increase a user's usage limits for the remainder of the day without changing his or her permanent account settings.

Open/Close Hours

This feature allows you to specify the times you would like your hotspot to be active. For example, you might not want to have the hotspot on while your business is closed.

Walled Garden

You can add websites to a list that users can visit before they log in and register. For example, suppose that you want all users to register before they use the Internet; however, you want to give them easy access to your company website. Therefore, you would just add your company domain (yourcompany.com) to the walled garden list.

Firewall

Use Public IP to configure the firewall rules to protect your network from malicious activities. Open and close ports as needed, and configure access to computers on your local network. ZoneCD allows you to configure your wireless signal to block or limit access to your wired network. By default, private (wired) LAN access is blocked from hotspot users. (However, the Super user class has access to the entire network.) You can also allow access to your entire wired network, or define a specific IP address and ports to allow access to a single or multiple computers on your network.

Reports

Many reports are available, such as usage, limits and blocks, and another for the content filter. You can apply date ranges and filter results by username, MAC address, or IP address. You can also group the data by username, MAC, or IP if you want to see more cumulative data. All reports also generate bar graphs and pie charts. You can also view summary reports for the number of logins per day and time-of-day usage for the past four weeks so that you can get an idea of your busy times.

Ticket System

A ticket system is available if you want to disable self-registration for the hotspot users and generate automatically chosen logins to be printed and distributed to visitors. The ticket has the network name, username, ticket valid date and time, and a brief message from you (optional).

This allows you to have more control over who uses the hotspot. Suppose you notice that some people are using the free hotspot but are not purchasing your products within your store. To remedy that, you can start giving hotspot access to only paying customers. You can set up the ticketing system and hand out the login information at the front counter or cash register.

Network Availability Hours

Unlike the open/closed feature, the network availability function allows you to define when your hotspot is available for each hour of each day. This is a nice feature to keep users off your network during closed hours or busy times.

Spot Check

A Rich Site Summary (RSS) feed is available to monitor the usage and availability of your hotspot. While inside Zone Control, the same data is available from the status page from within a Flash object. Watch active user sessions and system loads to always be on top of your hotspot. If a gateway fails, you are notified via RSS or a message in the Flash object, and the system also e-mails the details of the crash to your hotspot's support e-mail address. You are notified again upon recovery.

NOTE RSS typically syndicates news and other information online. You can enter the RSS feed address provided by ZoneCD into a reader, display, or device that interfaces with this type of feed, such as customized Yahoo or Google home pages.

Hotspot Directory

You can list your hotspot in the hotspot directory on the Public IP website. This provides additional marketing of your hotspot.

Network Printer

You can configure a shared network printer via Zone Control. If you provide an IP address of the printer, along with a small note to users, the printer (among other things such as available time, transfer, hours, and so on) will be displayed in the user's Connection Properties window upon login.

Configuration Queue

Implementing some configuration changes on your ZoneCD might require restarting a service or rebooting the gateway. After you have made any configuration changes in Zone Control, you can approve the updates. The changes are then downloaded to your gateway. A broadcast message is sent to users if the action might affect connectivity (Windows XP and Windows 2000 users). The update is made on the gateway within 5 minutes. You receive an e-mail response at your support e-mail address when configuration is complete.

Templates

Choose a template that is designed by Public IP, or, if you want more control, design your own. The template system uses the Smarty Template engine. If you decide to subscribe to a service that allows you to customize your template, you should become familiar with the Smarty syntax.

Customize E-Mails

You can customize the e-mails that the server generates and sends to your users. Welcome, Forgot Password, and E-Mail Validation e-mails can be customized by entering your message and using special tags to insert variable values such as name, username, and password.

Step 2: Gather the Necessary Items

Before beginning the installation, gather all the required items for the ZoneCD solution. The following sections discuss each item you need, and the last section lists the recommended products.

What's Required

The following hardware is required with the ZoneCD solution:

- A private wired or wireless router for the Internet connection/firewall
- A wireless router or access point for the public wireless access
- A computer with the following:
    - An Intel-compatible CPU
    - At least 128 MB of RAM
    - A bootable CD-ROM drive
    - A floppy drive or USB thumb/flash drive
    - Two Ethernet network interface cards (NICs)
- The ZoneCD disc

When looking for the equipment for this solution, keep in mind that you should use the recommended products mentioned in this chapter.

 TIP Most of the equipment you need should be available at local consumer electronics stores. You can also try searching Internet stores, such as Amazon.com and Buy.com.

Private Wired or Wireless Router

Figure 5-5 shows where the router is placed in the solution.

Figure 5-5   Router Placement Example

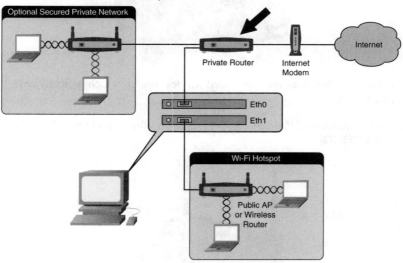

If you do not have an existing network at your location, you need to purchase a wireless or wired router. As pointed out in Figure 5-5, this router connects to your Internet modem and to the back of the ZoneCD computer.

No specific features are required for the wired or wireless router. You just need to use a standard wired router or a Wi-Fi-compliant wireless router.

This router enables you to easily create a private network, if desired. If you do decide to create a private network, take into account which router you should purchase. If you plan to have wireless coverage on the private network, use a wireless router. Otherwise, use a wired router. Keep in mind that you can use a wired router and later plug in access points to provide private wireless access. In addition, use a wired router if you do not plan to create a private network.

If you do have an existing network, and you have an available Ethernet port on the back of a wireless or wired router, you can plug into that instead of purchasing another one.

Figure 5-6 shows the recommended wired router, which typically costs between $40 and $90.

Figure 5-6   Recommended Wired Router: Linksys EtherFast Cable/DSL Router with Four-Port Switch (Model #BEFSR41)

Figure 5-7 shows the recommended wireless router, which typically costs between $25 and $70.

Figure 5-7   Recommended Wireless Router: Linksys Wireless-G Broadband Router (Model #WRT54G)

Public Access Point or Wireless Router

Figure 5-8 shows where the wireless access point or router is placed in the solution.

Figure 5-8   Placement Example of the Wireless Access Point or Router

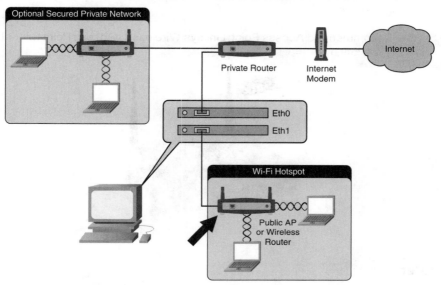

This piece of equipment, as pointed out in Figure 5-8, provides the public wireless access for the hotspot solution. You can use either an access point or a wireless router.

No specific features are required for the access point or wireless router. They just need to be Wi-Fi-compliant.

Figure 5-9 shows the recommended wireless router, which typically costs between $25 and $70.

Figure 5-9   Recommended Wireless Router: Linksys Wireless-G Broadband Router (Model #WRT54G)

Figure 5-10 shows the recommended access point, which typically costs between $60 and $80.

Figure 5-10   Recommended Access Point: Linksys Wireless-G Access Point (Model #WAP54G)

Computer

Figure 5-11 shows where the dedicated PC is placed in the solution.

Figure 5-11   Dedicated PC Placement

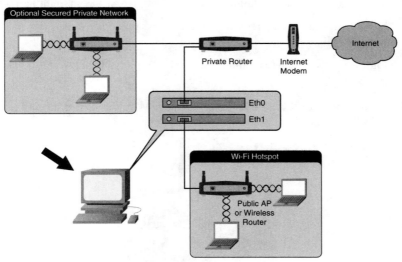

Make sure the computer you will use for the ZoneCD solution meets the requirements discussed earlier. The ZoneCD computer does not require an input/output device, such as a keyboard, mouse, or monitor, after the initial configuration is complete. To provide easier access when running headless (with no input/output devices), you can use Secure Shell (SSH) for remote administration of the system.

ZoneCD operates from a LiveCD; therefore, it cannot retain settings during a reboot. However, it has a system that saves the ZoneCD configuration and setting to a removable medium. Therefore, you need a floppy disk or a USB thumb/flash drive.

Figure 5-12 shows the recommended Ethernet NIC, which costs between $15 and $30.

Figure 5-12   Recommended Ethernet NIC: Linksys EtherFast 10/100 LAN Card (Model #LNE100TX)

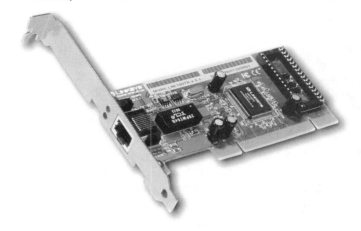

The ZoneCD Disc

Do not forget that you need the brains of this solution—the ZoneCD disc, which is included on this book's companion CD-ROM.

NOTE   This book's companion CD-ROM includes ZoneCD version 1.2-7.

If you download ZoneCD and burn your own CD, make a note of the version number. You'll probably need to reference it later.

You can also download the CD image (ISO file) free of charge from the Public IP website (http://www.publicip.net/zonecd/download.php).

You need to burn the ZoneCD ISO file to a regular CD-R disc. You can find help on the Public IP website, under the Development & Support section, on how to burn the file using several well-known CD-writing software packages.

You can also order a ZoneCD CD disc from Public IP for $10. This is good if you do not have a CD burner available, or you are not sure how to burn the ISO file onto a disc with your particular CD-writing software.

Set Up Your Zones (for the Free Service)

NOTE Follow the directions in this section if you will use the Closed mode and the free service; otherwise, disregard this section.

You need to create a few logins, or accounts, on the Public IP website. This allows you to use their Zone Control server. Creating these accounts also enables you to log into the web-based administration tools on the Public IP website.

First, you should create a master login. This lets you set up and create logins for your zones, or hotspots, each with a separate zone login. The zone login you create is required during the ZoneCD boot of that particular zone, or hotspot.

After you create and log into the master account, you complete a wizard that helps you configure and customize your zone. This wizard, called the Master Wizard, creates a template or "blueprint" that saves you the trouble of re-creating all the configuration options each time you add a new zone. If you have only one zone, or hotspot, to set up, this does not increase the time it takes to get set up. The wizard saves your answers and configurations in the Public IP database so that the Zone Wizard has these values when generating a new zone for you.

To start the process, create a master login:

1. Go to http://www.publicip.net/login.php.

2. In the Login dialog box, click the **New Master Account** link.

3. Enter your information and click the **Create Master Login** button.

4. You must activate the account by visiting the link contained in the confirmation e-mail.

5. After you log into the master account (see Figure 5-13 for an example), follow the Master Wizard. Then you need to create a zone by completing the Zone Wizard.

Figure 5-13 Example of a Master Account Web Page

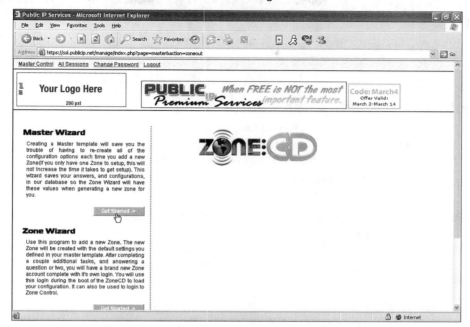

Set Up Your Zones (for the Premium Services)

NOTE Follow the directions in this section if you will use the Closed mode and purchase a premium service; otherwise, disregard this section.

First, you need to go to the Public IP website and sign up for a premium service by going to http://www.publicip.com/services.php.

After you complete the sign-up process and have activated your account, log on to the Zone Control. You might be taken automatically to the Zone Control login page after the account activation; however, you can log in by going to http://www.publicip.com and using the Login box in the upper-left corner of the website.

After you log in, complete the wizard, which serves as a template for setting up your zones, or hotspots. Then complete the wizard at the end to create a zone.

Step 3: Set Up and Configure the Access Points and Routers

The procedure in this step depends on whether you are using a private or public access point/router, as described in the following sections.

Private Wired or Wireless Router

If you do not already have an existing network (wired or wireless router), you should set up and configure your wired or wireless router after reading this section. See Figure 5-14 for a better idea of the piece of equipment being discussed. To set up your router, follow the manufacturer instructions that were included in the router product box. The instructions should have you connect the router to your Internet connection.

Figure 5-14   Placement Example of the Wired or Wireless Router

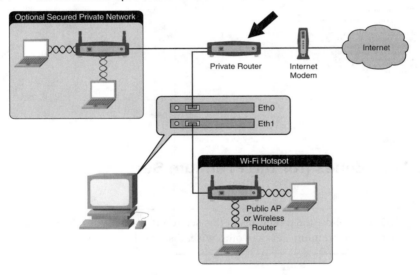

If you are setting up a wireless router (or a wired router and connecting access points) to provide wireless access for your private network, follow these steps to maximize your private network security:

- Use an encryption method, such as Wi-Fi Protected Access (WPA) or at least Wired Equivalent Privacy (WEP).

- Consider disabling Service Set Identifier (SSID) broadcasting, which helps hide your network from others.

- Configure a channel that's not being used by other nearby wireless networks, such as your Wi-Fi hotpsot. Software tools such as NetStumbler, which is included on the companion CD-ROM, or tools provided by some radio card manufacturers allow you to view information, such as channels, about your neighboring wireless networks. You should also try to use the nonoverlapping channels 1, 6, and 11. Try to avoid channel 6, however, because this is the default channel most wireless devices use; therefore, it's likely the most congested channel.

 NOTE Even though channel 6 is mentioned as the most congested channel, keep in mind that other electronic devices, such as cordless phones and microwave ovens, cause Radio Frequency (RF) interference with Wi-Fi devices.

If you suspect your Wi-Fi hotspot is being affected by RF interference, try using each nonoverlapping channel. See if there is any difference in connectivity or performance, because the interference might influence only certain channels.

- Make sure you set (or change the default) a password for your wireless router.
- You might not want to use a descriptive SSID (network name), such as the address or business name. This makes it harder for hackers to lock in the location of your network.

Public Access Point or Wireless Router

You should set up and configure your access point or wireless router after reading this section. See Figure 5-15 for a better idea of the piece of equipment being discussed.

Figure 5-15   Placement Example of the Access Point or Wireless Router

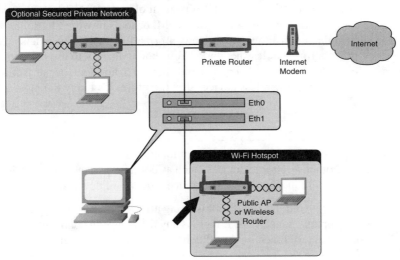

To set up your access point or wireless router, follow the manufacturer instructions that were included in the product box. However, the setup instructions for a wireless router usually have you connect it to the Internet connection. Do not connect the wireless router to the Internet modem; skip those steps. In addition, the setup instructions for access points might tell you to connect it to the network (via a router, switch, or hub); however, do not connect the access point to the network. The purpose of following the manufacturer instructions is just to set some initial settings, such as the network name and channel.

If you are using a wireless router, you must disable DHCP for your LAN before starting the installation. If you are using an access point for the public wireless access, do not worry about disabling DHCP, because access points do not have this feature; only routers do.

TIP   To disable DHCP, you probably have to access the router's wireless web-based administration utility after you set the initial settings. You can find out how to access this utility by looking in the wireless router manual or other included documentation. Keep in mind that when you are looking for the DHCP settings in the web-based admin utility, you will see a DHCP feature for the Internet connection. Do not mess with that; you need to disable the DHCP feature for the LAN.

NOTE DHCP is a feature that hands out IP addresses to devices (computers) that connect to the wireless router. Devices must have an IP address before they can access the Internet. Even though you disable DHCP on the wireless router, the user devices, such as laptops and PDAs, are assigned IP addresses from the ZoneCD system.

Either way you go (access point or wireless router), take into account a few things while configuring this piece of equipment:

- Do not use security or encryption methods.

- Use an SSID (network name) that describes the location and your intentions. For example, a café might use "Free Hotspot at Bob's Café." If the hotspot is being put in just for the local youth club, you might want to use "Youth Club Hotspot."

- Configure a channel that's not being used by other nearby wireless networks. Software tools such as NetStumbler, which is included on the companion CD-ROM, or tools provided by some radio card manufacturers allow you to view information, such as channels, about your neighboring wireless networks. You should also try to use the nonoverlapping channels 1, 6, and 11. However, try to avoid channel 6, because this is the default channel most wireless devices use; therefore, it's likely the most congested channel.

NOTE Even though channel 6 is mentioned as the most congested channel, keep in mind that other electronic devices, such as cordless phones and microwave ovens, cause RF interference with Wi-Fi devices.

If you suspect your Wi-Fi hotspot is being affected by RF interference, try using each nonoverlapping channel. See if there is any difference in connectivity or performance, because the interference might influence only certain channels.

- Use mixed mode so that users who are using either B or G wireless adapters can connect to your hotspot. This setting is chosen by default. So do not worry if you are not prompted to specify the mode.

Step 4: Perform a Physical Installation

To perform a physical installation, you need to complete the following steps:

1. If you have not already done so, you probably need to install at least one Ethernet NIC in your computer that will run the ZoneCD. Remember: You must have two Ethernet NICs installed in the computer, but the computer likely already has one. If it does not, you need to install two Ethernet NICs. To install the cards, follow the installation instructions that were included with the Ethernet NIC.

2. Connect an Ethernet cable to one of the Ethernet adapters on the back of the ZoneCD computer. (Refer to this as Eth1 for example purposes.) Then connect the other end of the cable to a LAN port on the back of the access point or wireless router, which will provide the public wireless access. Make sure you do not plug into the access point or wireless router WAN or Internet port.

3. Connect an Ethernet cable to the other Ethernet adapter on the back of the ZoneCD computer. (Refer to this as Eth0 for example purposes.) Then connect the other end of the cable to a LAN port on the back of your private wired or wireless router, which is connected to the Internet connection.

    This router should be running a DHCP server. If it is not, the ZoneCD must be assigned a static IP address during the boot process. DHCP is usually enabled by default.

4. Make sure the routers or access points are plugged in and the status lights are lit. In addition, ensure that the ZoneCD computer is plugged in.

Step 5: Perform ZoneCD Initial Setup

Now that you have connected the components, you need to go through the ZoneCD boot process and perform the initial configuration. If you have problems during the process, refer to the "Getting Help" section near the end of this chapter.

 TIP   If you are not familiar with using interfaces like the one used during the boot process, it might take some getting used to. You can use your keyboard arrow keys to move the cursor around and use the spacebar to select options. To accept your selection and move to the next screen, press the **Enter** key.

The Boot Process

The first task is to go through the boot process. The following steps let you know what should happen and what to expect during the ZoneCD boot.

1. Start your computer. After you have entered your operating system (such as Windows), insert the ZoneCD into the CD-ROM drive, and then restart the computer.

2. Just after the computer starts to boot back up, the CD should take over and start booting its software. You should see the boot splash screen with the ZoneCD logo, as shown in Figure 5-16.

Figure 5-16   ZoneCD Boot Splash Screen

3. During the boot, as shown in Figure 5-17, you will see messages going by on the screen.

Figure 5-17   Boot Messages

NOTE   If you are using a USB flash/thumb drive to save your configuration and it is not properly formatted, or if the disk or drive has an error, you are notified.

Select **Yes** to have the ZoneCD automatically partition and format the drive. Formatting the drive erases all existing data there.

If you do not want to lose the data on the USB flash/thumb, copy the files to your computer before continuing. You can also just use a floppy disk instead; if so, select **No**.

4. When the system has found (probed for) all the hardware to determine what hardware drivers to load, it displays the license agreement screen. See Figure 5-18 for an example. The license is based on the GNU CopyLeft license, which has been around for many years for open source software. This appears only when an unconfigured system is booting or during the first boot.

Figure 5-18   License Agreement Screen

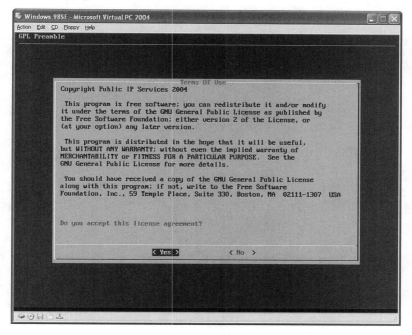

If you select **No**, the software halts the setup.

If you select **Yes**, the system proceeds with the bootup sequence.

This is the preamble to the GNU General Public License. This appears only during the first boot.

Select **Yes** to continue.

5. The screen in Figure 5-19 shows up on every boot, and you have only 5 seconds to respond.

Figure 5-19   Configure or Use Default Configuration Questionnaire Screen

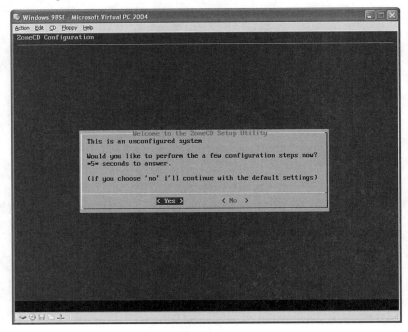

If this is your first boot, select **Yes**.

If this is not your first boot and you want to reconfigure the system, pop out the floppy disk that holds your saved configuration, and select **Yes**.

If this is not your first boot and you want to keep the saved configuration, just wait 5 seconds, and it will continue to boot.

If you do not select anything and it is your first boot, the ZoneCD automatically boots in Closed mode with DHCP enabled for your network configuration. If you did this by mistake, just restart the computer and start the process over again.

NOTE   If you have not inserted the floppy disk or connected the USB flash/thumb drive, you are prompted with a message. The ZoneCD cannot complete the boot process without the configuration media.

Stick the floppy in the drive or plug in your USB drive; then click **OK** to continue.

6. Select the mode, Open or Closed, that you want your ZoneCD to run in, as demonstrated in Figure 5-20.

Figure 5-20 Mode Selection Screen

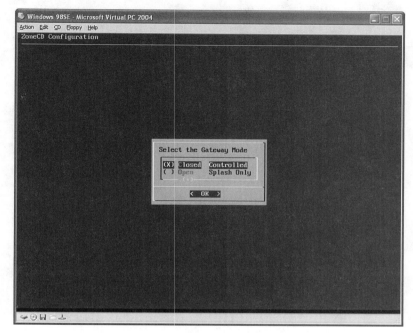

If you choose Closed mode, the screen next prompts you to select which server, Free or Premium, you want to use.

7. Select how you want the ZoneCD to run after setup is complete from the screen illustrated in Figure 5-21.

Figure 5-21 Interface Selection Screen

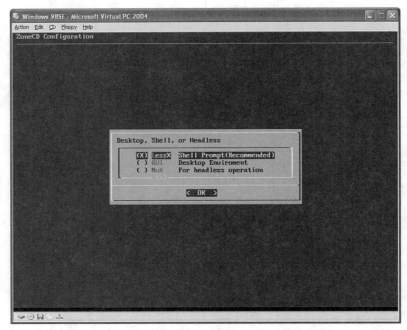

LessX—This starts only the X server and a single rxvt session—no window manager. This is done because the ZoneCD boots to runlevel 5; without the rxvt session, you get a broken shell (no job control).

GUI—Non-Linux geeks will probably be the most comfortable with GUI. This gives you a basic desktop with a web browser within the Linux operating system.

NoX—Use this if you plan to run the ZoneCD headless (no monitor, keyboard, mouse, and so on) after setup is complete.

8. Select the way you want to configure the network for the private side of the ZoneCD computer from the screen shown in Figure 5-22.

Figure 5-22   Private Side Configuration Selection Screen

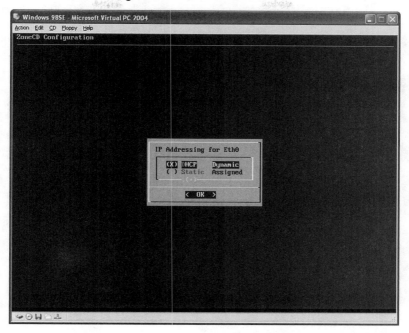

If the private wired or wireless router (which should be connected to the Internet) has DHCP enabled, select **DHCP**.

If you are not sure how the IP addresses are given out on the wired or wireless router, check with someone who knows. If you are not sure and you have not changed many settings on the router, you could probably guess that it has DHCP enabled, because this is set by factory default.

If the private wired or wireless router does not have DHCP enabled, select **Static** and follow these steps:

a   Enter an IP address to assign to the ZoneCD system.

b   Enter the subnet mask to use. Unless you have some special network setup, 255.255.255.0 should work.

c   Enter the IP address of the gateway. Most likely, this is the IP address of the private wired or wireless router (typically 192.168.1.1 or 192.168.0.1).

d   Enter the IP address of the primary name server. Again, this is probably the IP address of the private wired or wireless router (typically 192.168.1.1 or 192.168.0.1). You can also use the IP address of your ISP name server.

e Enter the IP address of the secondary name server. This is optional; if you do not have a secondary name server, or if you are not sure, just leave it blank.

9. Select whether you want to enable the automatic reboot feature from the screen shown in Figure 5-23.

Figure 5-23 Reboot Selection Screen

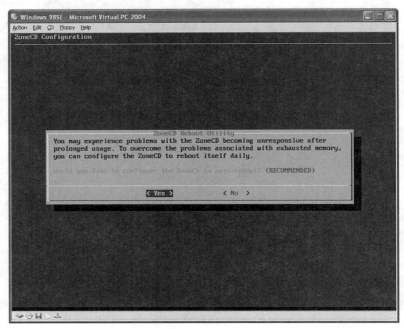

Because ZoneCD does not install to your hard drive, the file system is mounted on a RAM disk. Therefore, after a while, you might experience problems when you have utilized most or all of the RAM.

NOTE During reboots, the ZoneCD system should seamlessly go through the boot process and load your saved configuration information from your floppy disk or USB flash/thumb drive. Rebooting should not require you to do anything to get back to normal operation; however, you should manually reboot once, just to make sure it loads flawlessly.

If you do not want to enable the auto-reboot and would rather reboot manually on occasion, select **No**.

To help keep the ZoneCD memory resources optimized, select **Yes**, and then follow these steps:

a The ZoneCD uses UTC time (also known as GMT) to synchronize its activities. Select your location.

b Select your time zone or city.

c Select the time you want the reboot to happen.

You are almost done!

You should now continue with one of the following sections that correspond with the mode (and server type) you chosen

- Open mode configuration
- Closed mode (free server) configuration
- Closed mode (premium server) configuration

Open Mode Configuration

If you selected ZoneCD to run in Open mode, proceed with the following steps:

1. From the screen shown in Figure 5-24, enter a URL to redirect your users to after they click the button on the splash screen.

Figure 5-24 Redirection URL Selection

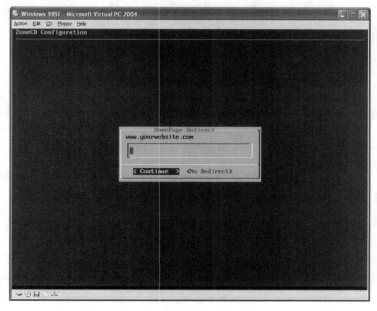

2. If you do not want your users to be redirected, select **No Redirect**, or just refrain from typing anything, to have them go to their normal home page (set within their browser) after the hotspot splash screen.

3. From the screen shown in Figure 5-25, you need to specify whether you want the content filter active.

Figure 5-25   Content Filter Selection

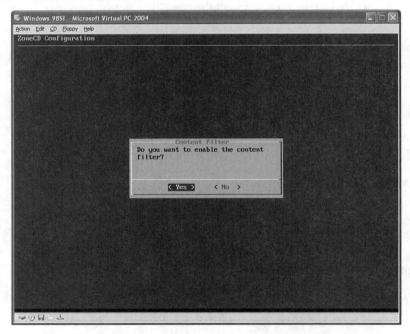

After you finish the Open mode configuration, a screen displays the configuration summary, and the boot should continue automatically. You see several messages that update your system. When you are taken to the interface you chose earlier, your hotspot is alive and ready for users.

Congratulations! You are all done!

Closed Mode (Free Server) Configuration

If you choose to run in Closed mode using the Free Server, proceed using the following steps:

1. Enter the login you created for your zone on the screen shown in Figure 5-26. Remember that these usernames and passwords are case-sensitive.

Figure 5-26　Login Input Screen

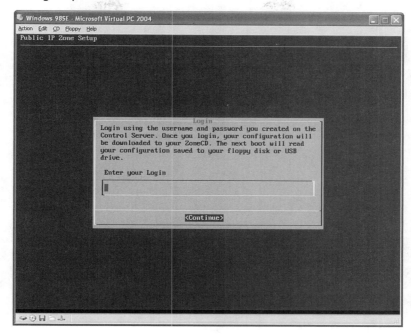

Closed mode requires that you have already created a Zone login. This is necessary for you to download your configuration from the remote server and to send and receive updates from the Control server.

NOTE　You cannot use a Master login (using an e-mail address) to boot ZoneCD; you must use the Zone login for the particular zone you are setting up.

2. Enter your password on the screen shown in Figure 5-27. This is a special dialog box that does not display what is typed, so concentrate when entering the password.

Figure 5-27   Password Input Screen

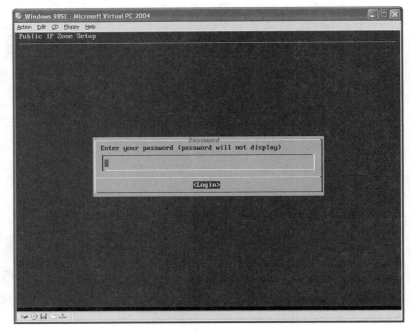

3. After your login information is validated, your configuration settings are downloaded from the Control server. After ZoneCD downloads the configuration information from the server, you should be taken to the interface you chose earlier. After that, your hotspot is alive and ready for users.

That's all! You are finished!

Closed Mode (Premium Server) Configuration

If you choose to run in Closed mode using the Premium server, proceed with the following steps.

NOTE   Make sure you saved the certificate key (you received it by e-mail from Public IP) to your disk or USB flash/thumb drive, following the directions in the e-mail. If you mess up, you can restart the computer to go through the boot process again.

After the steps in the previous section, the boot process, you should have seen the configuration summary. Then you can continue with these steps:

1. Enter the login you created for your zone on the screen shown in Figure 5-28. Remember that these usernames and passwords are case-sensitive.

Figure 5-28   Login Input Screen

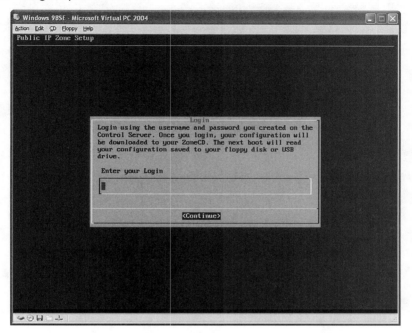

Closed mode requires that you have already created a Zone login. This is required for the to download your configuration from the remote server and to send and receive updates from the Control server.

NOTE   You cannot use a Master login (using an e-mail address) to boot ZoneCD; you must use the Zone login for the particular zone you are setting up.

2. Enter your password on the screen shown in Figure 5-29. This is a special dialog box that does not display what is typed, so concentrate when entering the password.

Figure 5-29 Password Input Screen

ZoneCD should continue to boot into the interface you chose earlier. After it does that, your hotspot is alive and ready for users.

Congratulations! You made it!

Check for Proper Operation

After you install your Wi-Fi hotspot, you should check that the system is actually working as intended and check if the intended coverage area is indeed covered.

Take a while to "play" with the system, and see if it works correctly. Then you should check for successful operation throughout the entire coverage area to ensure you are getting the amount you want. You can do this by moving to different locations throughout the facility with a laptop while monitoring the connection status, signal strength, and speed, as indicated by your wireless-equipped laptop. Be sure to actually make use of the Internet connection by continually browsing the web as you check the coverage areas.

If you find you aren't getting the coverage you want or if you want, to cover a large area, such as a hotel, you should refer to Chapter 12, "Increasing Your Hotspot's Wireless Coverage," for more information.

What's Next

After your ZoneCD computer boots into the interface you chose earlier, your hotspot should be operational. However, you should give it a try. Use a Wi-Fi-capable computer nearby, connect to the hotspot, and see if it works.

You do not change settings or view stats directly from ZoneCD; rather, you use the online admin tools, which are discussed next, if you are in Closed mode. If you are using Open mode, you cannot really change any of the settings; just reboot the computer and reconfigure the system.

If you need to reboot (after a power outage, for example), the ZoneCD system should automatically complete the boot process and load your saved configuration information from your floppy disk or USB flash/thumb drive. You should not have to do anything to get back to normal operation.

Using the Online Administration Tools

After you have everything set up and you want to view the status and settings of your zones, use the web-based admin tool (called Zone Control) on the Public IP website.

You can log into Zone Control using either the Master login or the login of a particular zone. When you log in with the Zone login, you are not allowed to change the zone's configuration and you have access to only user permissions, registration, and reporting. However, if you log on using the Master login, you can alter the characteristics of your zones. This allows operators to give the location staff limited access to Zone Control.

For FreeNet hotspots (using Closed mode), log into Zone Control at http://ssl.publicip.net.

For premium service hotspots, log into Zone Control at http://www.publicip.com/.

Getting Help

Public IP hosts a discussion forum on its website (see Figure 5-30) to help you and other hotspot owners when you experience problems or issues with the ZoneCD solution. You can also use the forum to recommend features for future ZoneCD releases, share your success stories, and more.

Figure 5-30   Public IP Discussion Forum

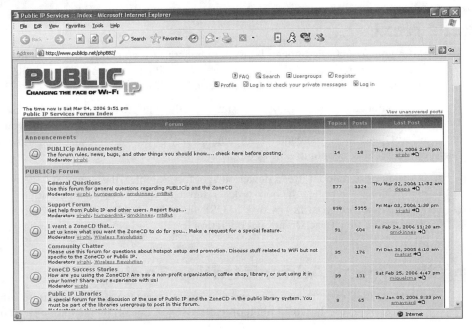

The discussion forum was put into place for people who are using the free services it is not particularly monitored for premium subscriber problems. However, premium users might still find help on the forums, but that is not guaranteed; they should use the Public IP eSupport.

NOTE   As a good practice, before posting your questions on the forum, you should do some searching for the particular issue you are experiencing and try working out your problem using previous conversions.

Visit the discussion forum at http://www.publicip.net/phpBB2/.

The eSupport system (see Figure 5-31) allows you to submit "trouble tickets" for direct answers. You can also view the knowledgebase, where you can see a categorized listing of frequently asked questions. The troubleshooter tool can also help; it takes you on a step-by-step tour to find the solution for your issue.

Figure 5-31 Public IP eSupport

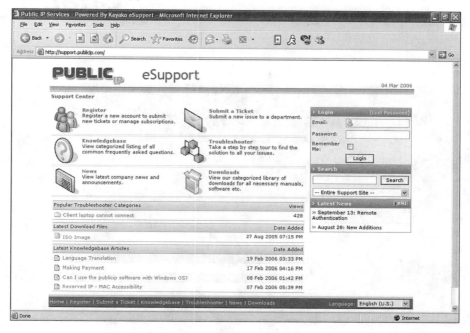

Visit the eSupport system at http://support.publicip.com/.

Chapter Review

The solution described in this chapter uses ZoneCD, a freely distributed LiveCD that is run from a dedicated PC, and a regular wireless router or access point, which makes this solution less expensive than other options.

Keep in mind the following things about ZoneCD:

- It provides many hotspot features.
- It has two modes in which it can operate: Open or Closed.
- Premium services are available if you want even more features and support.

Chapter 6

Solution 3: Join Boingo's Hotspot Network to Provide Paid Access

This solution allows you to be a part of Boingo Wireless, a huge hotspot network that provides paid access to thousands of on-demand and monthly subscribers. You purchase a specific wireless router and activate the Hot Spot in a Box feature.

Understanding the Solution

This solution, as depicted in Figure 6-1, works by setting up a wireless router connected to your Internet connection.

Figure 6-1   Network Layout Diagram

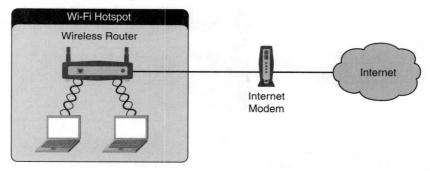

After you complete the sign-up process, your wireless router will be a Boingo hotspot. As shown in Figure 6-1, hotspot users wirelessly connect to the wireless router. After the hotspot user tries to access the Internet, the router intercepts him and requires him to register or log into the Boingo Wireless hotspot network before he is allowed to freely browse the web.

Setting Up the Solution

The overall steps to complete when setting up this solution are as follows:

Step 1   Gather the necessary items.

Step 2   Set up the equipment.

Step 3   Join Boingo's hotspot network.

Step 4   Perform the physical installation.

The next sections help you perform each step.

Step 1: Gather the Necessary Items

Before you begin the installation, gather all the required items for your solution.

For the Boingo hotspot solution, the only required piece of equipment is the hotspot gateway, as shown in Figure 6-2. This router typically costs from $120 to $160.

Figure 6-2   Wireless Router (Linksys Wireless-G VPN Broadband Router: Model WRV54G)

 TIP   The equipment you need for this solution usually is not available at local consumer electronics stores. You should try searching Internet stores, such as Amazon.com and Buy.com.

Step 2: Set Up the Equipment

Before stringing wires around and mounting the equipment, set up and configure the equipment in a staging area, such as your office. Later, in Step 4, you will find the optimal location for the gateway and perform the actual physical installation.

Set up the wireless router by following the manufacturer instructions that were included in the router box. You will probably have to use a CD to set up the wireless router. The instructions should have you connect the router to your Internet connection and go through a setup wizard.

Following are tips and comments you should refer to during the setup wizard:

- Do not use security or encryption methods.
- Configure a channel that other nearby wireless networks are not using. Software tools such as NetStumbler, which is included on the companion CD, or tools provided by some radio card manufacturers allow you to view information, such as channels, about your neighboring wireless networks. You should also try to use the nonoverlapping channels of 1, 6, and 11. However, try to avoid channel 6, because it is the default channel that most wireless devices use; therefore, it is likely the most congested channel.

TIP   Even though channel 6 is mentioned as the most congested channel, keep in mind that other electronic devices, such as cordless phones and microwave ovens, cause radio frequency (RF) interference with Wi-Fi devices.

If you suspect that your Wi-Fi hotspot is being affected by RF interference, try using each nonoverlapping channel and see if connectivity or performance is different, because the interference might influence only certain channels.

- Use mixed mode so that users who have either B or G wireless adapters can connect to your hotspot.

Step 3: Join Boingo's Hotspot Network

After you complete the initial setup, join Boingo Wireless and activate Hot Spot in a Box. Your wireless router should have come with specific instructions on how to sign up. The instructions should have you sign up through a page on the router web-based configuration utility, similar to that shown in Figure 6-3.

Figure 6-3   Example of the Boingo Sign-Up Page

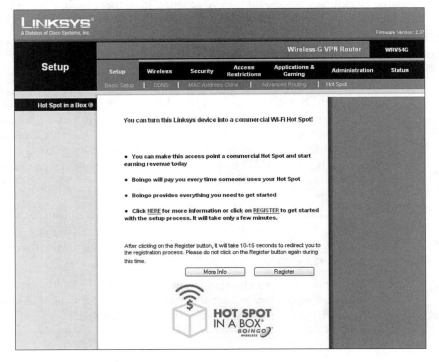

Step 4: Perform the Physical Installation

You can now begin installing your equipment.

NOTE   Given the layout of this book, this section and the entire chapter help you through the process of setting up only a single wireless router. A single wireless router provides only a limited coverage area. If you desire more coverage—such as to provide access for more than just a hotel lobby, small group of rooms, or café—you likely need to refer to Chapter 12, "Increasing Your Hotspot's Wireless Coverage," after completing this chapter.

Placing the Wireless Router

When finding a place to install the wireless router, do the following:

- **Think about the intended coverage area**—The wireless router should be as close as possible to the hotspot's intended coverage area, and preferably in the middle.

  For example, a motel owner might want to provide access to only a specific group of guest rooms, as shown in Figures 6-4 and 6-5. The owner should try to center the wireless router as much as possible, as shown in Figure 6-4, rather than as shown in Figure 6-5.

Figure 6-4 Example of a Good Wireless Router Placement

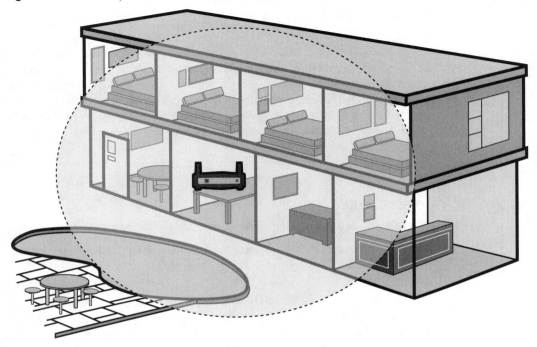

Figure 6-5   Example of a Less Desirable Wireless Router Placement

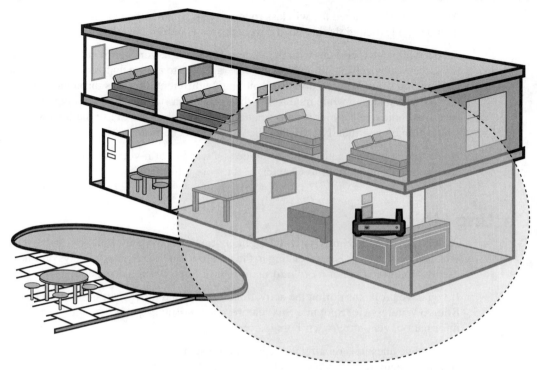

- **Locate near the Internet connection**—The wireless router should be near the Internet connection. The quality of the signal going through the Ethernet cable lessens as it travels; therefore, you should try to reduce the amount of cable needed to wire the gateway to the Internet. If required, you can typically move your Internet connection to accommodate a better placement of your router.

- **Keep equipment secured**—The equipment should not be exposed to the public. Public access makes it possible for someone to inadvertently or purposely move the antennas or vandalize the system.

- **Plan for the future**—Think about optimal locations if you are planning to run Ethernet cables to access points from the wireless router. For more information, refer to Chapter 12 after completing this chapter.

Check for Proper Operation

After you have installed the wireless router, check whether the system is working as intended and whether the intended coverage area is indeed covered.

Take a while to experiment with the system and see if it works correctly. Then check for successful operation throughout the coverage area to ensure that you are getting the amount you want. You can do this by moving to different locations throughout the facility with a laptop while monitoring the connection status, signal strength, and speed, as indicated by your wireless-equipped laptop. Be sure to use the Internet connection by continually browsing the web as you check the coverage areas.

If you find you aren't getting the coverage you wanted, or if you want to cover a large area, such as a hotel, refer to Chapter 12 for more information.

Getting Help

As with any other technology, you will likely run into problems with your hotspot. If you have problems or issues relating to the wireless router and other Linksys products, use its support team. For more information, visit http://www.linksys.com.

If you have problems during the activation or setup, and other issues related to the Boingo Wireless Hot Spot in a Box feature, use the Boingo support team. For more information, visit http://www.boingo.com.

If you have questions relating to the general hotspot installation, or if you need additional help, refer to Chapter 11, "Common Problems and Fixes," for more resources.

Chapter Review

Hotspot solution 3 allows you to potentially earn additional revenue by joining Boingo Wireless. Being part of such a huge hotspot network makes it more likely that your visitors will be willing to pay for Internet access.

In addition, this hotspot solution will likely provide the most publicity, because you will be listed in a hotspot directory that Boingo users use to find hotspot locations.

With this solution, you purchase a typical small office wireless router and simply activate the Hot Spot in a Box feature.

Chapter 7

Solution 4: Free or Paid Access and Private Network Using Hotspot Gateway

This solution provides an easy way to integrate or create a private network with your public network (hotspot) using a single Internet connection. The D-Link Airspot Wireless G Hot spot Gateway (DSA-3200) has both public and private ports to ensure that your private and confidential information is secured from the public. You can set up this solution several different ways, depending on your wants and needs.

Understanding the Solution

This solution, as depicted in Figure 7-1, works by setting up a hotspot gateway connected to your Internet connection. Then you can hook up your existing or new network devices to the back of the gateway to provide the Internet access for your secured private network.

Figure 7-1   Network Layout Diagram

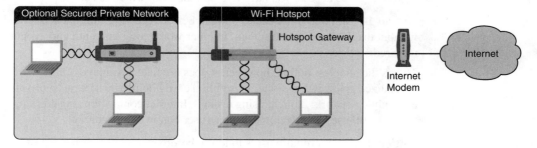

As shown in Figure 7-1, hotspot users can wirelessly connect to the gateway. When the hotspot users try to access the Internet, the gateway intercepts them and might require users to register or log in, depending on how you set it up, before they are allowed to freely browse the web.

If you apply usage limits, such as bandwidth or time limitations, the gateway enforces them and takes action when needed. For example, say that a user purchases one hour of hotspot access, valid anytime within the next 30 days. The gateway keeps track of session usage times and cuts off the user access when one hour of accumulated access has been accounted for or after 30 days, whichever comes first.

Setting Up the Solution

Complete the following steps to set up this solution:

Step 1 Choose the particular solution.

Step 2 Gather the necessary items.

Step 3 Set up the equipment.

Step 4 Configure additional settings.

Step 5 Perform the physical installation.

The next sections help you through each step.

Step 1: Choose the Particular Solution

Depending on the type of access you want to provide, you can implement the overall solution in various ways. The main differences among these options, which are discussed later, are if and how the users will create accounts to access the hotspot.

Free Access Options

When providing free access, you have five options from which to select:

- **Option 1**—Do not require users to log in before receiving Internet access and without displaying a splash screen. In other words, user authentication is not required.

  This is the simplest option; however, it does not take advantage of the specialized gateway functions. This option easily helps you separate a private and public network, though, using a single Internet connection. In addition, you can still use some features, such as user bandwidth limitation.

- **Option 2**—Do not require users to log in before receiving Internet access; however, they see a splash screen before they can freely access the Internet by using an external RADIUS server.

- **Option 3**—Require users to log in before receiving Internet access by manually inputting the usernames and passwords for the hotspot users into the web-based configuration tool.

  This is the most cost-effective option if you know you will have few users or less frequent users needing accounts. For example, this option is good if you are setting up a hotspot for a youth club or in other situations in which you will not need to add user accounts often. Keep in mind that your users can also have a shared username and password. This way, you need to create only one user account for many or all of the users.

- **Option 4**—Require users to log in before receiving Internet access by using the compatible ticket printer to physically hand out automatically generated usernames and passwords.

  This is a good option if you want to give hotspot access to only a particular group of people. For example, you might want to offer free hotspot access only to paying customers.

- **Option 5**—Require users to log in before receiving Internet access by using an external RADIUS server to handle online account creation by the hotspot users via the splash screen.

  This option provides an easier way to monitor the users' hots pot activity and enables you to display a splash screen for advertisements or to display localized user-friendly information.

Paid Access Options

When providing paid access, you have three different options from which to select:

- **Option 1**—Physically accept cash or credit cards from users, and then manually input the usernames and passwords for the hotspot users into the web-based configuration tool.

  This may be the least expensive option to provide paid wireless Internet access; however, it's not very practical if you plan to receive many users.

- **Option 2**—Physically accept cash or credit cards from users, and then use the compatible ticket printer to physically hand out automatically generated usernames and passwords.

  This is a more practical way to provide paid access without the hassle of setting up a RADIUS server.

- **Option 3**—Accept online payments from hotspot users via your hotspot's splash screen by using an external RADIUS server.

  This is an ideal option to implement if you want to provide paid access, because users can make payments without interacting with the administrator or owner.

NOTE If desired, you can implement multiple options. For example, even if you use the ticket printer, you can manually input user account information. You can usually do the same if you are using a RADIUS server.

You can also follow option 3 to accept online credit card payments and use a ticket printer so that users can pay you with cash or some other physical payment.

TIP Setting up your own RADIUS server takes time and technical expertise. Finding a company that provides this service via remotely located RADIUS servers already set up for hotspot user authentication and payment processing is likely much easier. The later section "RADIUS Server" provides some information about these companies.

Choose the option(s) that best fit your particular situation, and continue with the next step.

Step 2: Gather the Necessary Items

Before beginning with the installation, gather all the required items for your solution. This particular solution might involve these three items:

- A hotspot gateway
- A ticket printer
- A RADIUS server

The following sections discuss each item in greater detail.

TIP The equipment you need for this solution usually is not available at local consumer electronics stores. Try searching Internet stores, such as Amazon.com and Buy.com.

Hotspot Gateway

The only required piece of equipment for this solution is the hotspot gateway, as shown in Figure 7-2. A hotspot gateway typically costs from $480 to $700. The prices vary so much because some gateways come with ticket printers.

Figure 7-2   Airspot Wireless G Public/Private Hot Spot Gateway (DSA-3200)

Ticket Printer

If you choose one of the options that require the ticket printer, you need to get the compatible printer, as shown in Figure 7-3. A ticket printer typically costs from $300 to $400. As mentioned before, ticket printers are sometimes included with the gateway.

Figure 7-3   Airspot Ticket Printer (DSA-3100P)

RADIUS Server

If you are choosing to implement an option that uses a RADIUS server, you can either purchase and set up an actual server, which can cost thousands of dollars and take a considerable amount of time, or you can subscribe to a service that offers hosted servers. Many different companies, such as the following, offer hosted RADIUS services for as low as $20 to $50 per month:

- **WirelessOrbit**—http://www.wirelessorbit.com/
- **ALEPO**—http://www.alepo.com/
- **Pronto Networks**—http://www.prontonetworks.com

NOTE A convenient list of companies that offer hosted RADIUS services, such as in the preceding list, is available at the companion website (http://www.wifihotspotbook.com/bonus_materials/).

Step 3: Set Up the Equipment

Before stringing wires around and mounting the equipment, you should set up and configure the equipment in a staging area. Later, in Step 5, you will find the optimal location for the gateway and perform the actual physical installation.

Hotspot Gateway Setup

Set up the gateway by following the manufacturer instructions (that is, Quick Installation Guide) that were included in the box. The instructions should have you connect the gateway to your Internet connection and go through the setup wizard on the web-based configuration utility. Take into account the tips and comments provided in this book about some of the default features and settings in the wizard.

Figure 7-4 shows an example of the first page you see after logging into the web-based configuration utility. This is where you start the setup wizard.

Figure 7-4　　Example of the Main Page of the Gateway Web-Based Configuration Utility

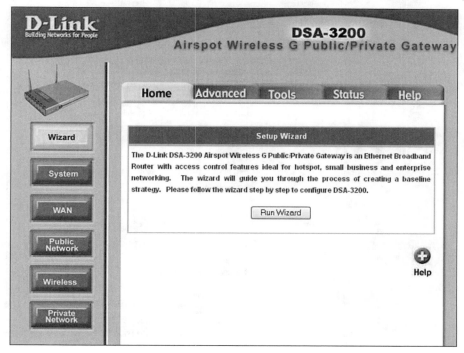

Here are the tips and comments you should refer to during the setup wizard:

- Do not use security or encryption methods for the public wireless access.
- Use a service set identifier (SSID) that describes your business, organization, or attentions (basically, a network name). For example, a café might use "Free Hotspot at Sams Cafe," as shown in Figure 7-5. If the hotspot is being put in just for the local youth club, you might want to use something such as "Youth Club Hotspot."

Figure 7-5 Example of Setting the SSID of Your Gateway

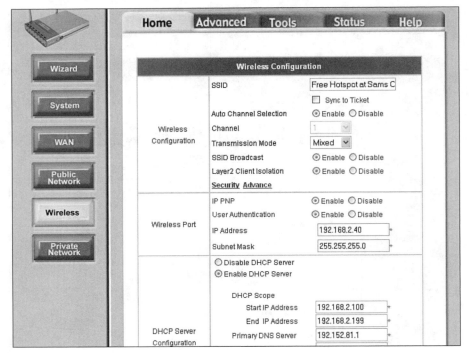

■ Configure a channel that other nearby wireless networks are not using. Software tools such as NetStumbler, which is included on the companion CD, or tools provided by some radio card manufacturers allow you to view information, such as channels, about your neighboring wireless networks. If you use the auto channel selection feature, the router automatically selects the least congested channel. However, if you want to define a specific channel instead, use one of the nonoverlapping channels, which are 1, 6, and 11. However, try to avoid channel 6, because that is the default channel that most routers and gateways use; therefore, it is likely the most congested channel.

NOTE Even though channel 6 is mentioned as the most congested channel, keep in mind that other electronic devices, such as cordless phones and microwave ovens, cause radio frequency (RF) interference with Wi-Fi devices.

If you suspect that your Wi-Fi hotspot is being affected by RF interference, try using each nonoverlapping channel to see if connectivity or performance is different. The interference might influence only certain channels.

- Use mixed mode so that users who have either B or G wireless adapters can connect to your hotspot.

You will configure all the other gateway settings in Step 4.

Ticket Printer Setup

Set up the ticket printer by following the manufacturer instructions (that is, Quick Installation Guide) that were included in the product box. The instructions should have you connect the printer to your gateway and should point you to the section in your gateway's web-based configuration utility to configure the settings for the ticket printer, as shown in Figure 7-6. You can refer to the gateway product manual for details on the settings.

Figure 7-6   Example of the Ticket Printer Settings Section in the Gateway Web-Based Configuration Utility

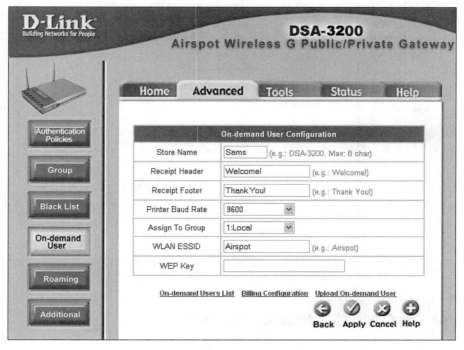

RADIUS Server Setup

If you will be using a RADIUS server, such as to handle authentication, you should configure the settings in the section of the gateway's web-based configuration utility that deals with authentication policies, as illustrated in Figure 7-7.

Figure 7-7   Example of the Authentication Policies Section in the Gateway's Web-Based Configuration Utility

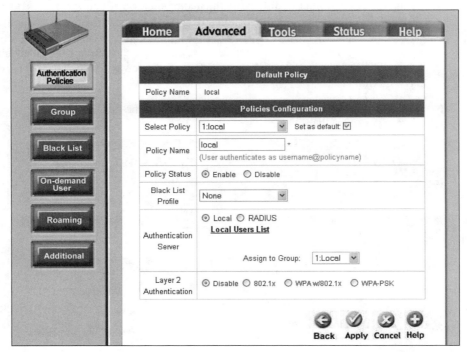

You should refer to the instructions of your RADIUS server or service provider and the gateway's product manual for the setup and configuration information.

Step 4: Configure Additional Settings

Even though you completed the wizard, you still need to configure many more settings. Go through all the configuration screens on the gateway's web-based configuration utility so that you understand all the settings and features. To help you understand these features and settings, refer to the gateway manual.

NOTE   In most cases, manuals are not included in the box with wireless networking products. Instead, you can download product manuals from the websites of these manufacturers. For the gateway product manual, go to http://www.d-link.com, and refer to the Support section.

As you read through the manual, follow along on your gateway web-based configuration screens and make any required or desired changes. Take into account the following tips and comments about certain features and settings:

- **DoS Protection for User**—The recommended practice is to enable this feature, because it helps provide a safer and more secure experience for your hotspot users.

- **DHCP Settings**—Unless you are an experienced system administrator, leave the DHCP default settings for all the network interfaces (public wireless, public LAN, and private LAN).

- **SSID Broadcast**—The recommended practice is to enable SSID broadcasting, because hotspots are made to be open to the public.

- **Layer 2 Client Isolation**—The recommended practice is to enable this feature because it helps provide a safer and more secure experience for your hotspot users. However, if you want the public users to be able to communicate (for example, to share files), you need to disable this feature. Keep in mind that you should understand the risks involved.

- **Security**—You should not use security or encryption methods, such as WEP or WPA, for the public wireless access.

Step 5: Perform the Physical Installation

Now you can start with the physical installation of your equipment.

NOTE   Given the layout of this book, this section and the entire chapter help you through the process of setting up the gateway and its accessories, such as the ticket printer. The gateway alone provides a small coverage area. If you need more coverage, such as to provide access for more than just a hotel lobby, small group of rooms, or a café, you likely need to refer to Chapter 12, "Increasing Your Hotspot's Wireless Coverage," after completing this chapter.

Placing the Gateway

When you are looking for a place to install the gateway, do the following:

- **Think about the intended coverage area**—The gateway should be as close as possible to the hotspot's intended coverage area, and preferably in the middle.

  For example, a motel owner might want to provide access to only a specific group of guest rooms, as shown in Figures 7-8 and 7-9. The owner should try to center the gateway as much as possible, as shown in Figure 7-8, rather than as shown in Figure 7-9.

Figure 7-8   Example of a Good Gateway Placement

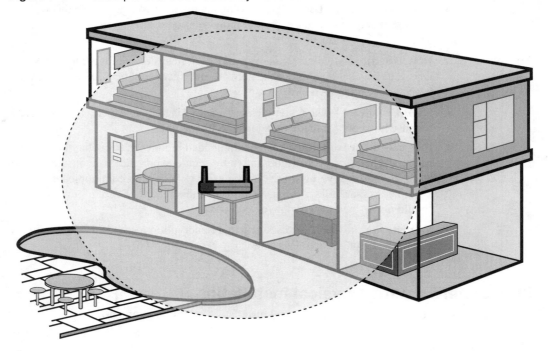

Figure 7-9   Example of a Less Desirable Gateway Placement

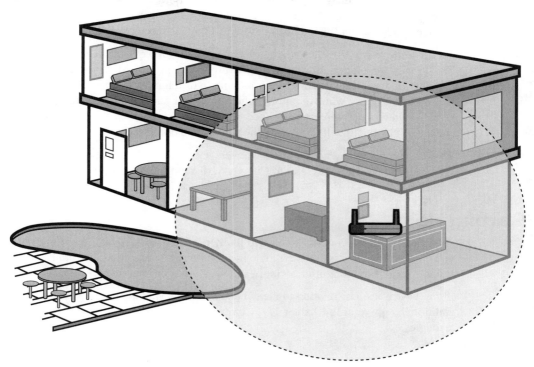

- **Locate near the Internet connection**—The gateway should be near the Internet connection. The quality of the signal going through the Ethernet cable lessens as it travels; therefore, try to reduce the amount of cable needed to wire the gateway to the Internet. If required, you can typically move your Internet connection to accommodate a better placement of your gateway.

- **Think about accessories**—If you are using a ticket printer, it must be within a few feet of the gateway.

- **Keep equipment secured**—The equipment should not be exposed to the public.

- **Plan for the future**—Think about optimal locations if you are planning to run Ethernet cables to access points from the gateway. For more information, refer to Chapter 12 after completing this chapter.

Check for Proper Operation

After you have installed the gateway, check whether the system is actually working as intended and whether the intended coverage area is indeed covered.

Take a while to experiment with the system and see if it works correctly. Then check for successful operation throughout the coverage area to ensure that you are getting the amount you want. You can do this by moving to different locations throughout the facility with a laptop while monitoring the connection status, signal strength, and speed as indicated by your wireless-equipped laptop. Be sure to actually use the Internet connection by continually browsing the web as you check the coverage areas.

If you find that you are not getting the coverage you wanted, or if you want to cover a large area, such as a hotel, refer to Chapter 12 for more information.

Getting Help

As with any other technology, you will likely run into problems with your hotspot. If you have problems or issues relating to the gateway and other D-Link products, use its support team. For more information, visit http://www.d-link.com.

If you have questions relating to the general hotspot installation, or if you need additional help, refer to Chapter 11, "Common Problems and Fixes," for more resources.

Chapter Review

Hotspot solution 4 allows you to provide free or paid wireless Internet access. It uses a real hotspot gateway, which makes this the most expensive solution. However, the gateway provides many benefits, such as these:

■ You can easily integrate or create a private network with your public network (hotspot) using a single Internet connection.

■ You can hand out hotspot login information via a ticket printer. This allows you to easily offer paid access by accepting payment using existing methods, such as your cash register, or offer "controlled free access."

■ You can use RADIUS servers or hosted services to enable better management of multiple hotspots.

Part III: **After Your Wi-Fi Hotspot Is Alive**

Chapter 8   Getting the Word Out

Chapter 9   Fending Off Freeloaders

Chapter 10   Wi-Fi Safety and Security

Chapter 11   Common Problems and Fixes

Chapter 12   Increasing Your Hotspot's Wireless Coverage

Chapter 13   Using Wi-Fi Networks

Chapter 8

Getting the Word Out

The saying "If you build it, they will come" does not exactly fit with Wi-Fi hotspots. Even though people might see your hotspot pop up on their laptop in the available network list, you should promote your hotspot. We are not talking about huge advertising campaigns; instead, we are talking about plopping some simple stickers on your doors or windows and spending some time in front of the computer listing your hotspot in online directories. This helps expand the use of your hotspot and increase the number of customers who visit your establishment.

Signage

A great way to let your visitors know that you have a hotspot is to display a "Wi-Fi Here" sign or sticker on your front window or door. This helps catch public attention when people pass by your location. Another great way to promote your Wi-Fi hotspot is by placing tent cards on your tables and desks. For example, if your business is a café, you might want to place the cards on the eat-in tables and by the cash register to ensure that all your visitors know about your hotspot. This is also a way you can inform visitors of the details, such as the network name and pricing information.

You can go about acquiring signage in several ways:

- Get the signs from an organization such as Boingo, which provides marketing materials when you become a partner
- Purchase them
- Create your own

If you joined the Boingo hotspot network, you will likely receive a marketing kit that contains, among other things, ready-to-use stickers and tabletop tent cards. It is highly recommended that you use these items.

If you cannot obtain ready-to-use signage, you can create your own. It is fairly easy to make your own signs, and you can create some neat-looking stickers with supplies from your local office supply store.

For signs, you can use just use plain white paper. To be more attractive, you can experiment with different colored and designed papers. To make window stickers or decals, you can purchase and use special paper or clear plastic sticker sheets that you can print on. Explore your local office supply store for materials.

As far as the text for the signage you create, you can use well-known phrases such as "Wireless Internet Access" or "Wi-Fi Hotspot Here." Of course, if you are offering free access, you definitely want to mention that on the sign. If you create a large-enough design, you can also add some details about the hotspot. For more artistic touches, you can add photos or clip art of related items, such as laptops or PDAs.

You can use familiar images from organizations such as the Wi-Fi ZONE program. The Wi-Fi Alliance licenses the use of its trademarked logo (see Figure 8-1) to Wi-Fi ZONE providers. To become a zone provider, you have to use Wi-Fi certified equipment in your hotspot.

Figure 8-1   Wi-Fi ZONE Logo

Figures 8-2 and 8-3 provide some examples of Wi-Fi hotspot signage.

Figure 8-2   Large Sample Design

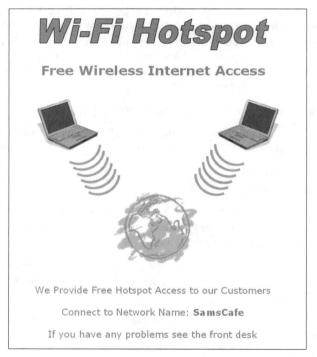

Figure 8-3   Small Sample Designs

NOTE   You can find downloadable "Wi-Fi here" sign and decal templates on the companion website for this book at http://www.wifihotspotbook.com/bonus_materials/.

Advertisements

If your business or organization runs advertisements or newsletters, you should mention that you provide wireless Internet access. This is a great way to get your hotspot publicized using existing channels. It costs only a little extra time or thought to somehow highlight your hotspot in an advertisement about your particular business or organization. For example, a hotel can add the words "Free Hotspot" to its regular advertisement in a travel magazine.

Keep in mind that you should also ensure that any internal members of your organization or business are notified of the newly installed hotspot. In addition, it is good if they understand the gist of how the hotspot works. They need to know how to use it and be able to explain the operation to potential users. A restaurant waiter, for instance, might need to explain to patrons how to connect to a hotspot located in the restaurant.

Online Hotspot Directories

Submitting your hotspot to online directories gives you the opportunity to receive visitors who otherwise probably would not have found your location. People all over the world can find your hotspot by searching online directions. They can view the details of the hotspot, such as the address of the location, the service set identifier (SSID), and the type (free or paid).

To get a better idea of the user experience when searching for your and others' hotspots, see Figure 8-4, which shows the results (from a popular online hotspot directory) of a search for hotspots in a particular area.

Figure 8-4 Hotspot Search Results

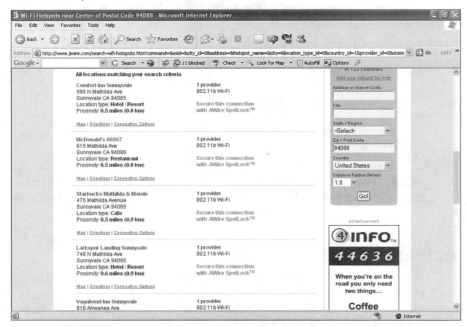

After the user browses through the list of hotspots, he can click a particular entry for more details, as shown in Figure 8-5.

Figure 8-5   Hotspot Directory Entry Details

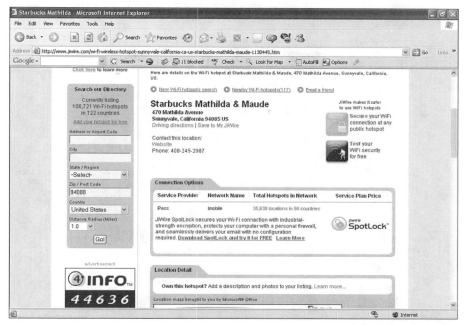

Some directories might even have an integrated mapping feature, such as that shown in Figure 8-6, so that users can easily find where the hotspots are located. Also shown in Figure 8-6, this hotspot directory (and maybe others) allows you to add a custom description and photos of your location for the public to see. This can help your hotspot stand out from other hotspots in the area.

Figure 8-6   Hotspot Directory Entry Mapping Details

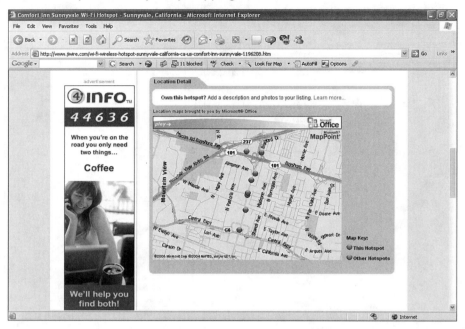

Table 8-1 lists many different hotspot directories to which you should submit your hotspot information.

Table 8-1   *Online Hotspot Directories*

Name	Website
JiWire	www.jiwire.com
Wi-Fi Zone	wi-fi.jiwire.com
Wi-FiHotSpotList.com	www.wi-fihotspotlist.com
Wi-Fi-FreeSpot Directory	www.wififreespot.com
Wi-Fi 411	www.wifi411.com
The Hotspot Haven	www.hotspothaven.com
MetroFreeFi	www.metrofreefi.com
WiFinder	www.wifinder.com
Hotspot Locations	www.hotspot-locations.com

NOTE If you decide to join the Wi-Fi Alliance Wi-Fi ZONE program, it is recommended that you do this while joining the JiWire directory. During the sign-up process for JiWire, you will be asked if you want to join the Wi-Fi ZONE program. Joining both of them (if this is what you want to do) through one form saves time.

NOTE You can find a convenient list of online hotspot directories, such as those listed in Table 8-1, at the companion website for this book (http://www.wifihotspotbook.com/bonus_materials/).

Submitting your hotspot to online directories is fairly easy. The sign-up process and policies vary among the different directories; however, most have just a simple online form that you can fill out and submit. You will probably have to input information, such as the following:

- Your contact information (name, address, e-mail, and so on)
- Wireless technology (b or g)
- Usage terms (free or paid)
- The SSID (or network name) of the hotspot

Be sure to update your entries in online directories if your network changes.

Chapter Review

As discussed in this chapter, you can help increase the usage of your Wi-Fi hotspot and the exposure of your establishment by doing the following:

- Placing "Wi-Fi here" stickers or decals on your windows or doors
- Mentioning your hotspot in your advertisements
- Listing your hotspot in online directories

Chapter 9

Fending Off Freeloaders

Offering free Internet access is a convenient service for your customers and visitors; however, it also attracts freeloaders. If your goal in installing and operating a free Wi-Fi hotspot is to attract more customers to your location, you should try to prevent users from using your hotspot without taking advantage of your primary goods and services.

This chapter discusses different methods to prevent freeloading at free access hotspots.

Physically Hand Out Login Information

The most feasible way to ensure that only the people you want to use your free hotspot have access is to physically hand out the login information. You can accomplish this by requiring users to log in before they use the hotspot, and requiring that they receive the username and password from you, rather than being able to self-register via the hotspot splash screen.

The primary method to physically hand out login information is to use a ticket printer, such as in Solution 4 (covered in Chapter 7), used in conjunction with the hotspot gateway. The ticket printer is simple to set up and use. You define the amount of access time that you want to give users and the time limit for valid accounts. When everything is set up, press a button, and a receipt prints with all the hotspot information and the automatically generated username and password. Then simply hand the receipt to your customer or visitor.

Solution 2 using the ZoneCD also allows you to print receipts by using a regular printer. Although it is not as convenient to use and set up as a real ticket printer, as with the D-Link gateway solution, the ZoneCD provides similar features at a much lower cost.

Apply Usage Limits

You can apply several usage limits to help reduce freeloading of your Wi-Fi hotspot. These limits are good to implement even if freeloading is not a big concern.

Open/Closed Times

If your hotspot location closes during the night and freeloading is one of your concerns, consider closing your hotspot during nonbusiness hours. Doing so keeps people outside of your facility, such as in the parking lot, from getting access to your hotspot.

Most wireless routers (see Figure 9-1), hotspot gateways, and RADIUS server services (see Figure 9-2) allow you to define when you want to provide Internet access.

Figure 9-1   Example of the Open/Closed Settings in a Web-Based Configuration Utility for a Wireless Router

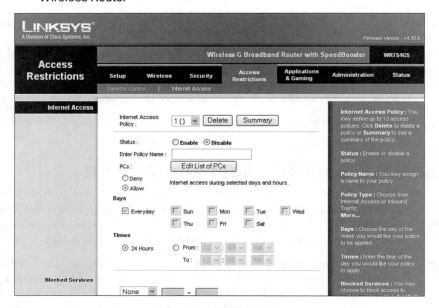

Figure 9-2   Example of the Open/Closed Settings in ZoneCD's Control Server

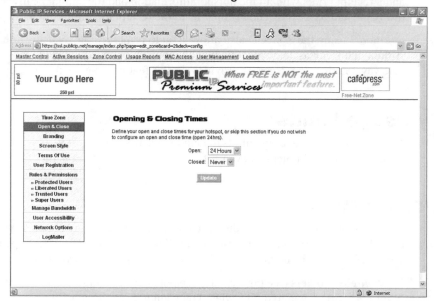

Bandwidth Limits

Setting user bandwidth limits can prevent users from having all the bandwidth of your Internet connection and evenly distributes bandwidth among all the users. Most hotspot gateways have this feature, and it is set via the device's web-based configuration utility, as shown in Figure 9-3.

Figure 9-3 Example of the Bandwidth Settings in a Web-Based Configuration Utility of a Hotspot Gateway

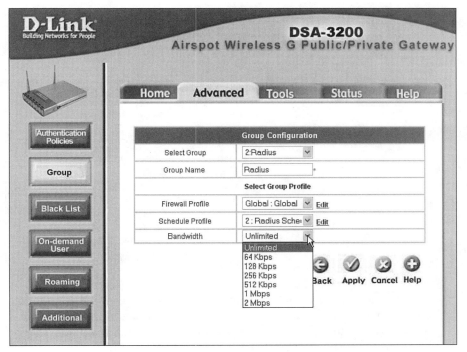

For example, suppose your cable connection to the Internet supports about 2 Mbps of bandwidth. Say that a user downloads a 10-MB attachment from an e-mail. During the download, with no bandwidth limits, he receives nearly all the 2-Mbps bandwidth, which would slow down other users who are competing for the bandwidth. With bandwidth limiting on and set to 500 Kbps, a few users can equally split the bandwidth of the Internet connection. Of course, the user who is downloading the attachment has to wait much longer to complete the download; however, it will not cause such a drastic effect on the other users.

Some hotspot gateways or RADIUS server services have other bandwidth limits, such as the amount of bandwidth a user can use over a specified period, such as in the ZoneCD solution and shown in Figure 9-4. This helps prevent users from downloading many files while using a hotspot. A hotspot owner might not want users to be constantly using a lot of bandwidth, such as downloading lots of files or attachments.

Figure 9-4   Example of the Bandwidth Settings in ZoneCD's Control Server

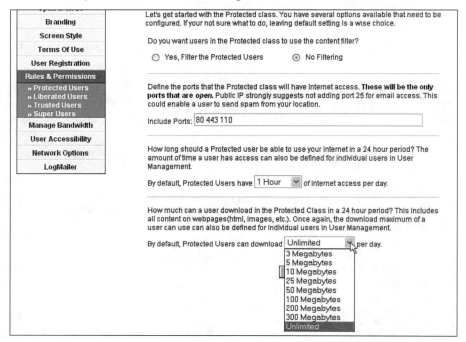

For example, a hotspot owner might impose a 10-MB bandwidth limit per day on all the users. Say that a user connects to the hotspot and spends half an hour checking e-mail and visiting websites, and he uses only 3 MB of bandwidth. Another user spends just 20 minutes on the hotspot, but he downloads many files and reaches the 10-MB bandwidth limit. Imposing a bandwidth limit per day helps equally distribute the Internet connection among users.

Spell Out Usage Terms

You should spell out the usage terms on your hotspot login or splash screens. To help fend off freeloaders, you could mention that the Wi-Fi hotspot service is provided only to customers of your business.

You should also mention other issues that you are concerned with, such as users spending too much time on the hotspot. For example, you might also mention in the terms that users should limit their use of the hotspot to an hour or less per day.

Monitor Your Hotspot

Monitoring your hotspot, such as the usage logs, helps crack down on freeloaders and is needed because you cannot always see the users of your hotspot. For example, people might be connecting to the hotspot from outside your facility, such as from the parking lot or in the apartment or office building next door.

If you are using a hotspot gateway or RADIUS server and you use user accounts, you can typically view the connection and usage details of each user, as shown in Figures 9-5 and 9-6.

Figure 9-5   Example of the Usage Logs in a Hotspot Gateway Web-Based Configuration Utility

Traffic History (2006-04-21)								
Date	Type	Name	IP	MAC	Pkts In	Bytes In	Pkts Out	Bytes Out
2006-04-21 02:31:14 +0800	LOGIN	egeier@local	192.168.2.143	00:14:BF:77:DE:83	0	0	0	0
2006-04-21 02:33:18 +0800	LOGOUT	egeier@local	192.168.2.143	00:14:BF:77:DE:83	362	295987	316	53781
2006-04-21 02:33:42 +0800	LOGIN	29E2@DSA-3200	192.168.2.143	00:14:BF:77:DE:83	0	0	0	0
2006-04-21 02:36:13 +0800	LOGOUT	29E2@DSA-3200	192.168.2.143	00:14:BF:77:DE:83	777	663760	683	119513
2006-04-21 02:36:48 +0800	LOGIN	TH83@DSA-3200	192.168.2.143	00:14:BF:77:DE:83	0	0	0	0
2006-04-21 02:48:18 +0800	LOGIN	egeier@local	192.168.2.171	00:02:2D:70:F8:EB	0	0	0	0
2006-04-21 04:31:34 +0800	KICK	egeier@local	192.168.2.171	00:02:2D:70:F8:EB	17826	20557643	14208	1906914
2006-04-21 04:35:55 +0800	LOGOUT	TH83@DSA-3200	192.168.2.143	00:14:BF:77:DE:83	7539	5247907	7544	1640282

Figure 9-6   Example of the Usage Logs in a RADIUS Server Web-Based Configuration Utility

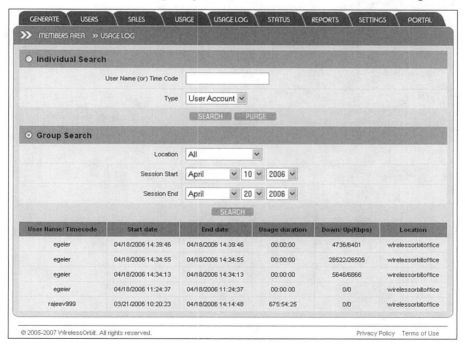

If you are using wireless routers or other devices that are not equipped with true hotspot features, or when you are not using user accounts, you can typically view the connection and usage details based on the DHCP IP or MAC addresses of the users.

If you do notice a freeloader, you can block him based on the user account, as shown in Figure 9-7, or by the MAC address(es), as shown in Figure 9-8.

Figure 9-7   Example of the User-Blocking Feature in a Hotspot Gateway Web-Based Configuration Utility

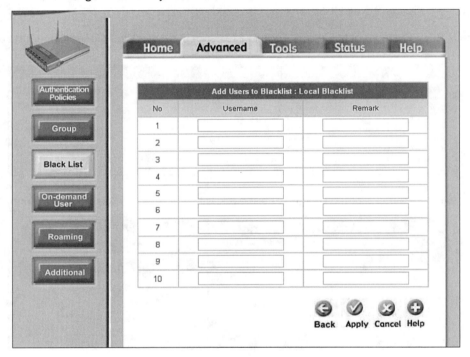

Figure 9-8 Example of the User-Blocking Feature in a Wireless Router Web-Based
Configuration Utility

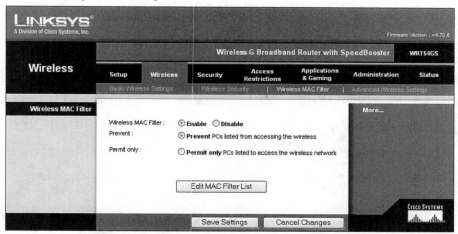

Chapter Review

This chapter discussed how to fend off hotspot freeloaders by using several different
methods:

- Physically handing out login information
- Applying usage limits
  - Open/closed times
  - Bandwidth limits
- Spelling out usage terms
- Monitoring your hotspot

Remember: The best way to prevent people from abusing your free Wi-Fi hotspot is to
physically hand out the login information. As discussed, this helps ensure that only
those you authorize are those who will be on the hotspot, and only for the amount of
time you specify.

Applying usage limits, such as open/closed times and bandwidth limitations, allows
you to prevent excessive use of your hotspot by users. These are good practices even if
you are not worried about freeloaders.

If you do not make it clear to the users what your usage terms are for the hotspot, you
will likely have many more freeloaders. Therefore, make sure the usage terms are
spelled out clearly.

After taking steps to prevent freeloaders, keep in mind that you should still monitor
your hotspot usage logs to ensure that people are not abusing your free Wi-Fi hotspot.

Chapter 10

Wi-Fi Safety and Security

Wireless technologies, including Wi-Fi, are subject to security issues because data is transmitted through the air. Because encryption methods are not utilized on hotspot networks, everyone within range can "listen in" or capture potentially sensitive data.

One of the main benefits of networking in general is the ability to share files among other network users. However, this is not such a desired feature on public networks, because the users probably do not want others browsing through their files.

This chapter addresses these issues and more, enabling you to provide a safer and more secure hotspot experience for your users.

Understanding Everyone's Responsibilities

Everyone has certain responsibilities when it comes to the safety and security of your Wi-Fi hotspot, as Table 10-1 illustrates.

Table 10-1 *Hotspot Administrator and User Responsibilities*

Hotspot Administrator/Owner	The User
Inform users of the risks when using a hotspot or unsecured wireless network.	Beware of the risks when using a hotspot or unsecured wireless network.
Give users safety and security tips.	Follow the safety and security tips.
Enable VPN[1] Passthrough.	Use VPN connections.
Isolate clients.	Disable file sharing.
Filter hotspot content.	Use personal firewall software.
Secure user information.	Keep an eye on valuables.

[1] VPN = virtual private network

Hotspot Administrator/Owner Responsibilities

You as the hotspot administrator or owner have the obligation to do many things to help ensure your hotspot users have a safe and secure experience.

Inform Users of the Risks

One of the most important responsibilities that you have as a hotspot administrator or owner is to ensure that your users understand the risks associated with using an unsecured wireless network, such as your hotspot. Following are three such risks:

- Internet activity can be monitored.
- Login information from unsecured Internet services and websites can be intercepted.
- Any shared files are open for others.

People who have the right tools can capture the data that is flying through the air. Because hotspots do not use encryption, all the information that is sent over the wireless network can be captured. This includes the usernames and passwords when logging into web-based applications, such as websites (that do not use Secure Sockets Layer [SSL] with a Hypertext Transport Protocol Secure [HTTPS] address), e-mail accounts, FTP connections, and other services that do not use encryption or other security methods.

Figures 10-1 through 10-3 show how a person can easily capture e-mail information on an unencrypted hotspot network.

Figure 10-1 shows an example of an important e-mail that a person might send from a hotspot.

Figure 10-1   E-Mail Sent from the Hotspot

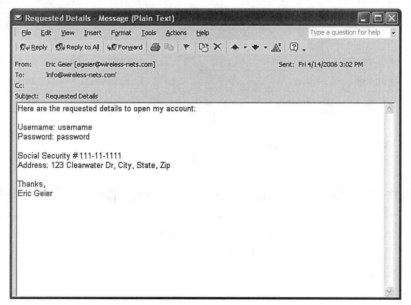

As shown in Figure 10-2, people who have the right tools might be able to retrieve your account details, including your username and password, when you synchronize your POP3 e-mail.

Figure 10-2   Real-Time Packets Captured Showing E-Mail Account Details

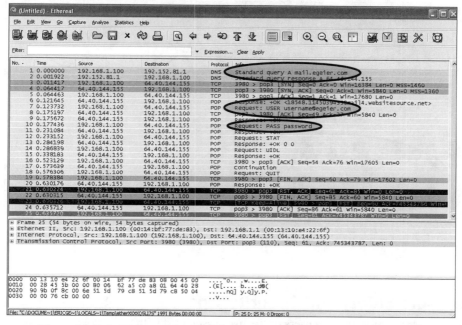

Figure 10-3 shows how others might even be able to see the contents of e-mails and the header information, such as the recipients of the e-mail.

People can also monitor the websites, and their content, that are visited through the wireless network. This might not be a huge concern for everyone; however, some people might want this information to be private.

Figure 10-3   Real-Time Packets Captured Showing the E-Mail Contents

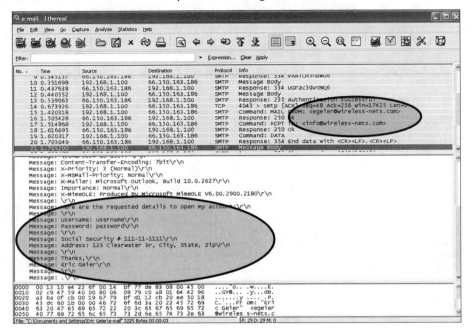

Give Users Safety and Security Tips

After informing the users of the risks associated with using your Wi-Fi hotspot, you should provide solutions or methods that will help limit or eliminate these risks and issues. These solutions, as shown in thefollowing list and discussed later, summarize the steps that users can take to ensure a safe experience while using public hotspots:

- Use virtual private network (VPN) connections.
- Use secure (SSL) websites.
- Disable file sharing.
- Use personal firewall software.

Enable VPN Passthrough

Users can use VPN connections to secure their information that is being passed through the public wireless network. In most cases, VPN Passthrough is enabled by default (and should not be disabled) on wireless networking equipment, such as routers, access points, or hotspot gateways. This Passthrough feature opens the ports that VPN connections use. You can find the Passthrough settings in the Miscellaneous or Security section of your wireless device configuration utility, as illustrated in Figure 10-4.

Figure 10-4 Example of VPN Passthrough Settings

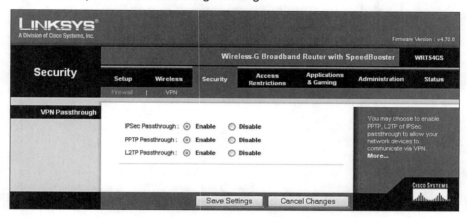

Isolate Clients

Some wireless devices, such as routers, access points, or hotspot gateways, have a client isolation feature, as shown in Figure 10-5. It is a simple and inexpensive version of the VLAN feature that is available on enterprise equipment. Client isolation blocks the traffic between the users on the network. Therefore, users cannot access each other's shared files. This benefits the people who forget to disable file sharing on their computer while using the hotspot.

Figure 10-5   Example of AP Isolation Setting

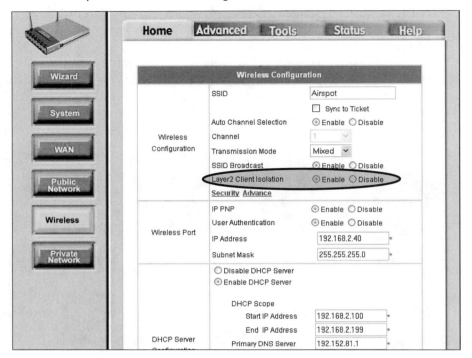

NOTE   Keep in mind that if your Wi-Fi hotspot uses multiple access points (APs), you should enable the client isolation feature for each AP. This is because the isolation feature can be implemented only on an AP-to-AP basis.

Filter Hotspot Content

You can use a few filtering methods to help keep your users safer while using your Wi-Fi hotspot:

- Filter web content (to block pornography, foul language, and so on).
- Block certain Internet ports (to prevent the use of file-sharing programs, POP3 e-mail, and so on).
- Block specific websites.
- Block websites based on keywords.

The filtering and blocking features of particular wireless routers and hotspot gateways vary greatly. See Figure 10-6 for an example of some filtering settings.

Figure 10-6 Example of Filtering Settings

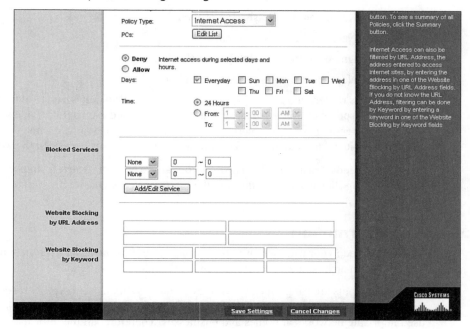

Web content filtering solutions allow you to easily block illegal or inappropriate websites. This solution is great for hotspots that might serve a majority of youngsters; however, it typically is not feasible for general hotspots. Actively filtering the websites that users visit typically requires the use of hardware, such as a proxy server, and is too expensive and time-consuming for most hotspot owners.

NOTE Keep in mind that the ZoneCD hotspot solution provides great web content filtering features and is convenient for places such as libraries and youth clubs.

Many wireless routers and gateways allow you to block users from using certain Internet ports. These ports are associated with certain applications and services, such as port 80 for web browsing.

Following are some ports you might want to block:

- **21**—FTP (prevent large transfers)
- **25**—SMTP Server (disable sending of POP3 e-mail to help prevent spam from originating at your hotspot)

- **445**—Prevent Internet hackers
- **1214**—Kazaa (online file-sharing program)
- **3689**—Network Jukebox protocol
- **6667**—Universal Internet Relay Chat (IRCU)
- **6699**—Napster (online file-sharing program)

Many wireless routers and gateways, as shown in Figure 10-6, allow you to block users from visiting specific websites or those that contain keywords you define. For example, if teens are spending hours on a certain website, and it is causing problems, you can add that website address to the list. This prohibits the teens from accessing the website.

Using these methods can also help protect you, as the hotspot owner, from users who are performing illegal activities through the Internet access you are providing.

Secure User Information

You should keep your user's information secure when it is traveling over the wireless hotspot and in any databases where sensitive information is stored.

Because hotspots are for public access, they usually do not use encryption methods—such as Wired Equivalent Privacy (WEP) or Wi-Fi Protected Access (WPA)—such as used in private networks at homes and businesses. Therefore, all the information that is passed through the wireless network is unsecured, and others can easily decipher the data. However, data that is sent to and from a website that uses SSL encryption, indicated by the padlock in the lower-right corner of the web browser and a web address of https, is safe and secure.

Therefore, to protect your user's information, use SSL encryption on all applicable web pages, which secures the login or payment information. Most hotspot gateways have this feature.

In addition, if you are using a RADIUS server or a hosted solution, you should look into and understand the security measures taken to keep the user information safe.

User Responsibilities

Even though you can take precautions to make your hotspot safer and more secure, it is up to the users to ensure their security.

Beware of the Risks

The saying "Ignorance is bliss" might come back to haunt people who ignore the risks and issues of using unsecured wireless networks such as hotspots. Even if users do not follow all the advice to limit or eliminate the risks, they should at least educate themselves. Therefore, when it comes to the safety and security of using Wi-Fi hotspots, the main responsibility of users is to be aware of the issues, as discussed earlier, so that they can properly protect themselves.

Follow the Safety and Security Tips

Hotspot users should follow any safety and security tips that you or others give them:

- Use VPN connections.
- Use secure (SSL) websites.
- Disable file sharing.
- Use personal firewall software.
- Keep an eye on valuables.

These items are discussed in the following sections.

Use VPN Connections

If users are conducting sensitive business, such as checking unsecured POP3 e-mail accounts via hotspots, they should use VPN connections to encrypt the information. Many businesses provide this service to their employees to access the corporate network while away from the office. Typically, VPNs securely connect remote networks or give people secure connections to a remote network. However, typical consumers can also use VPN connections to secure their hotspot experience. Even if your users do not intend to connect to remote networks, they might use VPNs because the information passed through the VPN tunnel is encrypted and secured from end to end.

NOTE   It is easy to set up a VPN server using Windows XP on a home computer. Alternatively, users can subscribe to a paid solution that hosts the VPN servers, such as JiWire's hotspot security solution. For more information about JiWire's hotspot security solution, visit http://www.jiwire.com.

Use Secure (SSL) Websites

When hotspot users are viewing sensitive information, such as web-based e-mail and banking information, they should ensure that the website is implementing SSL encryption on the website login page and during the entire sensitive session on the site. As discussed in a previous section, others cannot see the login and other information when SSL is in use.

Disable File Sharing

Before people use public hotspots, they should ensure that their PC has no actively shared files, folders, or other services. The sharing features that operating systems provide today are useful when using private networks; however, this is not the case when on public networks.

For more information about disabling file sharing, refer to Chapter 13, "Using Wi-Fi Networks."

Use a Personal Firewall

When using Internet connections, at home or on a public hotspot, users should use personal firewalls. Firewalls help prevent people from accessing your PC through the Internet. You can use operating systems, such as Windows XP, that have built-in firewall capabilities, or you can purchase software that provides the protection. Some hotspot-specific software solutions, such as the JiWire service mentioned earlier, provide firewall features. You can also look into consumer software titles, such as ZoneAlarm from Zone Labs or Kerio's Personal Firewall.

Keep an Eye on Valuables

Users should keep an eye on their valuables while using public hotspots, or others will. Users should keep items such as their laptop, PDA, or briefcase with them at all times.

Chapter Review

Given that Wi-Fi hotspots use the airwaves to transmit data and that they are used by the public creates many security issues. This chapter discussed ways to prevent and overcome many safety and security issues with public Wi-Fi hotspots.

Keep in mind the main concerns:

- Public Wi-Fi hotspots are inherently not secure. People who have the right tools can intercept the information that users send over the airwaves. However, users can take certain measures to protect themselves.
- Inform users of risks, and give them tips to stay safe and secure while using your public Wi-Fi hotspot.
- Enable features such as VPN Passthrough, client isolation, and web filtering to give users and yourself a safer hotspot experience.

Chapter 11

Common Problems and Fixes

As users begin to use your hotspot, you will likely have many connectivity and technical issues pop up. This chapter covers the main problems you might encounter and prioritized steps, for you and the users to perform, that will help fix them.

In addition to referencing this chapter when you have problems, you can use "cheat sheets" for quick access. This is especially convenient because you can post them at your location for the users and other members of the staff.

You can download common problems and fixes cheat sheets at http://www.wifihotspotbook.com/bonus_materials/.

Unable to See/Connect to the Wi-Fi Hotspot

Sometimes users cannot view your Wi-Fi hotspot in their available wireless network list or cannot connect to the hotspot.

What the User Should Do

This list details several actions that users can perform that might fix this problem:

- **Ensure that you are in the coverage area, and move closer to the Wi-Fi hotspot—** You might not be able to see or connect to the Wi-Fi hotspot because you are outside or on the fringe of the coverage area.

- **Check the radio card**—You might not be able to see the hotspot on your available wireless network list because your radio card is not enabled, or it might be jammed and not working properly.

  If your radio card is not enabled, enable it. If your radio card is already enabled, restart it by disabling it and re-enabling it. If you need help doing this, refer to Chapter 13, "Using Wi-Fi Networks."

- **Restart your PC**—Just like with any other computer problems, restarting the PC operating system clears up many problems.

What You Should Do

You can do several things as the hotspot owner or administrator to help resolve this issue:

- **Check the infrastructure device**—Users might not be able to view your network because the hotspot became unplugged. Therefore, ensure that the infrastructure device is plugged in and that the correct status lights are lit.

- **Restart the infrastructure device**—Unplugging the infrastructure device for several seconds and plugging it back in gives it a fresh start, which usually cures any weird quirks.

- **Restore the infrastructure device**—If you still cannot seem to see or connect to your Wi-Fi hotspot, you can try giving it a "hard reset" by restoring the infrastructure device to its factory defaults. This usually cures any problems associated with the infrastructure device.

  Most wireless routers, gateways, and other infrastructure devices have a small button (or tiny hole) on the back of the device for restoring. Although you should refer to your manual, typically all you have to do is hold the button in with a pen point or paperclip for up to 10 seconds.

CAUTION   You lose all the settings you have specified on the infrastructure device when you restore it to factory defaults.

- **Check for possible interference**—Other nearby wireless networks and devices, such as cordless phones and kitchen microwaves, that use the 2.4-GHz frequencies might interfere with your Wi-Fi hotspot and cause connectivity issues during their use.

  Do some experimenting to see if this is the cause of your problem. For example, when you experience connectivity issues, check whether anyone nearby is using other 2.4-GHz devices. If so, try to disable them and check whether you still have problems with your Wi-Fi hotspot.

  If you suspect that you are experiencing interference from other wireless devices, try changing your Wi-Fi hotspot channel.

Frequent Disconnections

Your hotspot users might experience an intermittent wireless connection to the Wi-Fi hotspot.

What the User Should Do

Users can do several things to try fixing an intermittent connection:

- **Move closer to the Wi-Fi hotspot**—Moving closer ensures that you are not on the fringe of the coverage area, causing your connection to be unstable.

- **Do not move around**—Walking or moving while connected to the hotspot might cause your connection to be unstable if you are in a partially covered area.

What You Should Do

Following are some actions you can take as the hotspot owner or administrator that might repair this problem:

- **Increase the hotspot coverage area**—If users are regularly losing their hotspot connections, you might want to think about increasing the coverage area.

- **Check for possible interference**—Other nearby wireless networks and devices, such as cordless phones and kitchen microwaves, that use the 2.4-GHz frequencies might interfere with your Wi-Fi hotspot and cause connectivity issues during their use.

  Do some experimenting to see if this is the cause of your problem. For example, when you experience connectivity issues, check whether anyone nearby is using other 2.4-GHz devices. If so, try to disable them and check whether you still have problems with your Wi-Fi hotspot.

  If you suspect that you are experiencing interference from other wireless devices, try changing your Wi-Fi hotspot channel.

Poor Performance

Users on your hotspot might experience poor performance, such as a slow Internet connection.

What the User Should Do

Following are several things users can try to solve poor performance issues:

- **Move closer to the Wi-Fi hotspot**—Moving closer ensures that you are not on the fringe of the coverage area, causing your connection to be unstable.

- **Do not move around**—Walking or moving while connected to the hotspot might cause your connection to be unstable if you are located in a partially covered area.

What You Should Do

You can do several things as the hotspot owner or administrator to help curb poor performance:

- **Check for possible interference**—Other nearby wireless networks and devices, such as cordless phones and kitchen microwaves, that use the 2.4-GHz frequencies might interfere with your Wi-Fi hotspot and cause performance issues during their use.

Do some experimenting to see if this is the cause of your problem. For example, when you experience connectivity issues, check whether anyone nearby is using other 2.4-GHz devices. If so, try to disable them and check whether you still have problems with your Wi-Fi hotspot.

If you suspect that you are experiencing interference from other wireless devices, try changing your Wi-Fi hotspot channel.

- **Implement bandwidth limiting, if available**—Enabling bandwidth limits on hotspot users helps ensure that everyone receives an equal part of the bandwidth, or speed, that the Internet connection provides.

  For example, suppose that your cable Internet connection averages about 2500 kbps. If no bandwidth limits are imposed, all the hotspot users will compete for the total bandwidth. Users who are downloading large files might adversely affect the bandwidth of other users, resulting in slower connections. With the bandwidth controls, however, you give only up to 250 kbps to each user, optimizing it for 10 users because 10×250 kbps = 2500 kbps. Now hotspot users are more likely to receive more reliable performance. The 250 kbps is not lighting-fast, but this should still be acceptable for just checking e-mail and web browsing.

  Keep in mind that you should set the bandwidth limits based on the average number of concurrent users you have on your Wi-Fi hotspot. For example, if you typically have only a few concurrent hotspot users, you can afford to provide them with more bandwidth, such as 800 kbps per user for an average of three users, or you might not even have to worry about limiting it.

- **Increase the hotspot coverage area**—If your hotspot users are regularly experiencing poor performance (possibly due to their location on the fringe of the coverage area), you might want to think about increasing the coverage area.

Internet Connection Unavailable

The hotspot user might be able to connect to the hotspot but might not be able to get to the Internet.

What the User Should Do

Users can do several things to help remedy their connection problem:

- **Check the IP address**—To access the Internet, your radio card must have a valid IP address assigned from the hotspot network. When you have a poor connection to the hotspot or when the network does not assign an IP address to your radio card, it usually gives itself an automatic private address, which is not valid.

  Move closer to the hotspot to ensure that you have a high-quality connection, and try reconnecting to receive a valid IP address so that you successfully access the Internet.

- **Restart the radio card**—Sometimes your radio card gets jammed and does not work properly. To fix a jam, disable and then re-enable your card. If you need help doing this, refer to Chapter 13.

- **Restart your PC**—Just like with any other computer problems, restarting the operating system clears up many problems.

What You Should Do

You have several options as the hotspot owner or administrator to repair connectivity:

- **Check the Internet modem**—Users might not be able to access the Internet because the modem became unplugged. Therefore, ensure that the Internet modem is plugged in and that the correct status lights are lit.

- **Restart the Internet modem and infrastructure device**—Sometimes your Internet modem and infrastructure device hang up and do not work properly. Simply unplug them for several seconds to give them a fresh start. It is typically recommended, and in some cases it might be necessary, to allow the modem to boot up before powering on your infrastructure device.

- **Restore the infrastructure device**—If you still cannot see or connect to your Wi-Fi hotspot, you can try giving it a "hard reset" by restoring the infrastructure device to its factory defaults. This usually cures any problems that are associated with the infrastructure device.

  Most wireless routers, gateways, and other infrastructure devices have a small button (or tiny hole) on the back of the device for restoring. Although you should refer to your manual, typically all you have to do is hold in the button with a pen point or paperclip for up to 10 seconds.

 CAUTION   You lose all the settings you have specified on the infrastructure device when you restore it to factory defaults.

- **Check with your ISP**—If your equipment is in working order and you still cannot access the Internet, your connection might be temporarily unavailable. You can usually call your Internet service provider (ISP) to see why your service is down and get a time frame for when service will return.

Where to Find More Help

If you cannot fix a problem by referring to this chapter, do not worry. You have other options for help:

- **Product manuals**—You should check the user manuals of the products for any troubleshooting information or advice that might help you solve your issue.

- **Manufacturer websites**—Keep in mind that most manufacturers offer online tools, such as knowledge databases and e-mail support, to help with issues relating to their products.

- **Manufacturer live support**—Some manufacturers also offer live online or telephone support for issues relating to their products. This is a great way to get some quick advice.

- **Discussion forums and e-mail lists**—To receive some independent guidance from others, you can try discussion forums and e-mail lists at websites such as http://www.wi-fiplanet.com.

- **Web searching**—Do not forget to prowl the Internet with your favorite search engine to see if you can find information on the web regarding the issues you are experiencing.

Chapter Review

Now you are armed with ways to combat some general issues you might run into while installing and operating your Wi-Fi hotspot. As you learn more about how Wi-Fi works and how your setup is operating, you will likely develop some intuition when it comes to wireless networks and be able to quickly troubleshoot problems down the road.

These are the main points to take away from this chapter:

- Ensure that you are within range of the hotspot.
- Ensure that all hardware is on (and plugged in when applicable) and working properly.
- If you are having problems that might be related to a single computer, remember that restarting the operating system might cure the problem.
- Wi-Fi uses the air to transmit and receive data; therefore, you must think about interference from other wireless devices.
- Do not forget about all the ways you can get help.

Chapter 12

Increasing Your Hotspot's Wireless Coverage

If you are not getting the desired wireless performance from your existing hotspot, or if you want to expand the coverage area or even cover your entire facility, you have a few options. These methods range from replacing an antenna to installing additional access points (APs) around your facility.

You can increase the wireless coverage area of your hotspot in three ways, as shown in Table 12-1.

Table 12-1 *Comparison of Methods to Increase Wireless Coverage*

Method	Amount of Coverage Increase	Cost	Difficulty
Use higher-gain antennas	Slight	Low	Easy
Use wireless repeaters	Moderate	Moderate	Moderate/high
Add APs	Unlimited	Moderate/high	Moderate/high

Keep in mind that you can implement a combination of these methods to achieve your desired coverage area. For example, you might want to cover a large portion of your facility. From the beginning, you might decide that you must install several more APs and that you will use high-gain omnidirectional antennas to maximize the coverage of each AP. After some investigating, you might find that it is pretty easy to wire a few APs around your facility; however, you cannot figure out how to run Ethernet cable to a part of the building. Therefore, you might decide to use wireless repeaters in this difficult area.

Higher-Gain Antenna

Although you will not see a huge increase in the wireless coverage area when you replace your wireless router or hotspot gateway "rubber duck" antenna with a higher-gain one, it is a good way to maximize the coverage area for that particular infrastructure device. It is also a good way to increase the signal strength for places that are already covered, resulting in better performance, as depicted in Figures 12-1 and 12-2.

Figure 12-1 Example of Coverage with a "Rubber Duck" Antenna

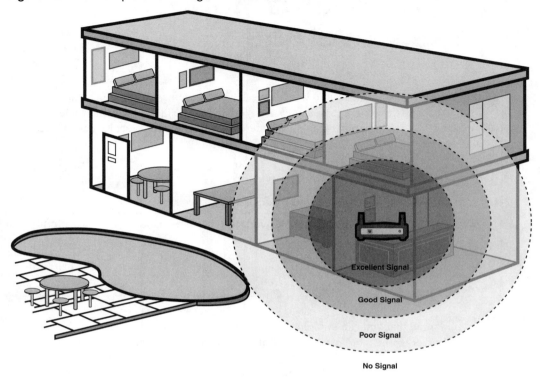

Figure 12-2   Example of Coverage with a High-Gain Antenna

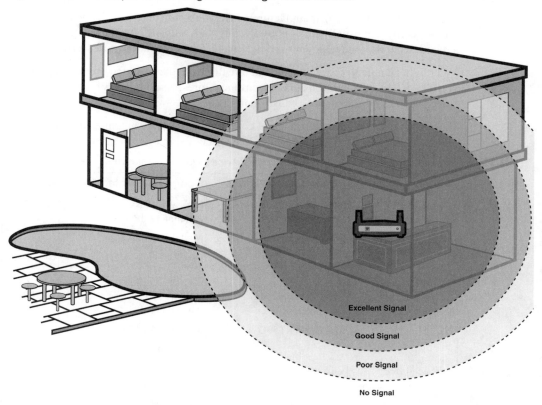

For example, say that a hotel manager sets up his hotspot gateway behind the front desk because that is where the Internet connection is. However, he wants to provide wireless Internet access to the people in the lobby and down the hall in the conference room. Hotel users often complain that they have a hard time keeping a connection to the hotspot in the conference room, and the typical signal strength is poor. He buys and hooks up a higher-gain antenna and then receives many fewer complaints about the coverage in the conference room, because the typical signal strength is now good.

NOTE   For more information about high-gain antennas, see the section "RF Propagation" in Appendix A, "Understanding Wi-Fi Signals."

Purchasing

Most wireless networking manufacturers offer high-gain antennas that work with their products. You can usually find out by visiting their website and browsing to their antenna section or viewing your product manual for compatible accessories.

You might be able to order the antenna directly from the manufacturer or a retailer. If you do not find it at local consumer electronics stores, you should try searching Internet stores, such as Amazon.com and Buy.com.

Table 12-2 lists the information about compatible high-gain antennas for the infrastructure devices used in the solutions discussed in this book.

Table 12-2   *High-Gain Antennas for Infrastructure Devices Used in Solutions*

Solution	Infrastructure Device	Compatible Antenna	Cost
Simple free access hotspot	Linksys Wireless-G Broadband Router Model #WRT54G	Linksys R-TNC Antenna (7 dBi) Model # HGA7T (sold in pairs) See Figure 12-3	$35–$60
Advanced free access hotspot using ZoneCD	Linksys Wireless-G Broadband Router Model #WRT54G	Linksys R-TNC Antenna (7 dBi) Model # HGA7T (sold in pairs)	$35–$60
Advanced free access hotspot using ZoneCD	Linksys Wireless-G Access Point Model #WAP54G	Linksys R-TNC Antenna (7 dBi) Model # HGA7T (sold in pairs)	$35–$60
Join Boingo's hotspot network to provide paid access	Linksys Wireless-G VPN Broadband Router with a 5-dBi Antenna Model # WRV54G	Linksys R-SMA Antenna (7 dBi) Model # HGA7S	$36–$50
Free or paid access and private network using hotspot gateway	D-Link Airspot Wireless G Public/Private Hot Spot Gateway with two 2-dBi Antennas Model #DSA-3200	D-Link 2.4-GHz Omnidirectional 7-dBi Indoor Antenna (need two) Model # ANT24-0700 See Figure 12-4	$35–$50 each

Figure 12-3   Linksys R-TNC 7-dBi Antenna (HGA7T)

Figure 12-4   D-Link 2.4GHz Omnidirectional 7-dBi Indoor Antenna (ANT24-0700)

Bear in mind that if you use a different brand from the infrastructure device for the antenna, you should buy an antenna that has the supported connector type.

Installation

To replace the antenna of your infrastructure device, you can usually remove the existing "rubber duck" antenna and connect the new antenna cable. Then you need to properly position the antenna and, if required, mount it. Generally, you get better performance if you position the antenna vertical to the ground. If the antenna has a separate base that you must mount, you can hide your infrastructure device, if desired, and place the antenna in a more visible location to obtain maximum range or coverage.

Wireless Repeaters

The use of wireless repeaters allows you to moderately increase the size of your Wi-Fi hotspot while not worrying about running Ethernet cables through your facility.

As depicted in Figures 12-5 and 12-6, you can install wireless repeaters in places where the signal is starting to fade away to provide access to users who are outside of the existing coverage area. The repeater picks up the fading signal and repeats it; therefore, users who are near the repeater can receive the signal. Of course, the user transmissions near the repeater are also picked up by the repeater and are repeated to a regular infrastructure device that is connected to the network or Internet connection.

NOTE Using wireless repeaters can reduce the total performance capacity of your network up to 50 percent. However, Internet speeds are typically much slower than the networks; therefore, you might not have to worry. Nevertheless, hotspot users might experience lower Internet speeds when the hotspot system uses repeaters. Be especially careful when using more than one or two repeaters and in situations where maximum performance is needed.

Figure 12-5   Example of Coverage Without a Wireless Repeater

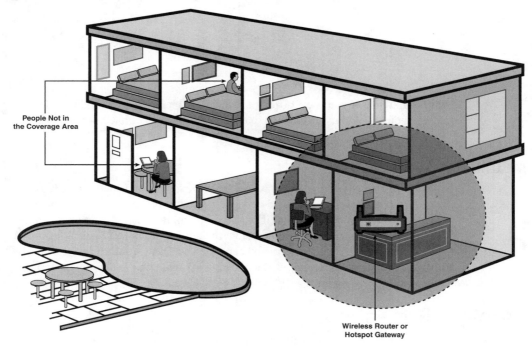

Figure 12-6 Example of Coverage with a Wireless Repeater

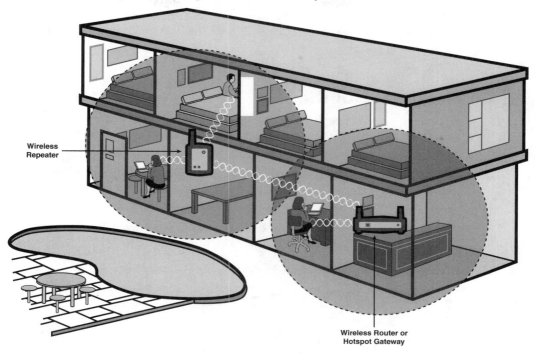

Purchasing

The equipment that you need for this solution usually is not available at local consumer electronics stores. To purchase a repeater, try searching Internet stores, such as Amazon.com and Buy.com.

Use the Wireless-G Range Expander (Model #WRE54G), shown in Figure 12-7. The typical cost of this wireless repeater ranges from $70 to $100.

Figure 12-7 Recommended Wireless Repeater: Wireless-G Range Expander (Model #WRE54G)

Installation

Set up the wireless repeater by following the manufacturer instructions (that is, the Quick Installation Guide) included in the box. The instructions might have you go through a setup wizard.

Adding Access Points

Expanding your Wi-Fi hotspot by adding APs mainly involves finding the right places to set up the APs within your facility and figuring out how to wire them back to the network.

APs are similar to wireless routers and hotspot gateways in the sense that they all provide wireless connections to end users. APs, however, do not provide routing or hotspot features, because these features are not needed.

Figures 12-8 and 12-9 illustrate the difference between a single wireless router or hotspot gateway network and an expanded network using APs.

Figure 12-8   Example of a Single Wireless Router/Hotspot Gateway Network

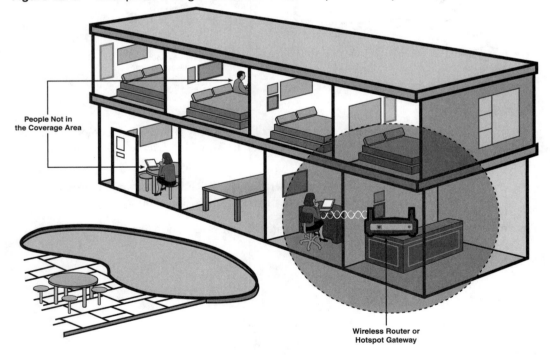

Adding APs to your hotspot network gives users a larger coverage area to make a wireless connection to one of the APs, which are connected to the main network, as shown in Figure 12-9.

Figure 12-9 Example of a Network Expanded with APs

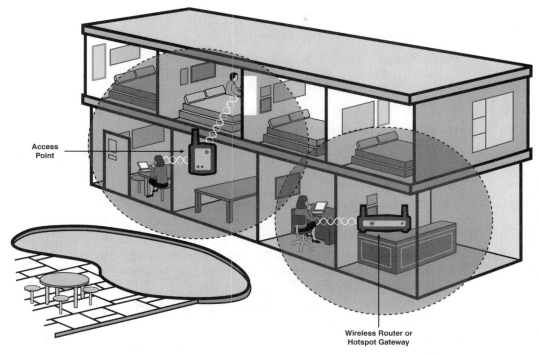

Access Point

Wireless Router or Hotspot Gateway

Preinstallation Site Survey

The first task when expanding your hotspot with multiple APs is to conduct a preinstallation site survey. This is necessary because with wireless systems, it is difficult to predict the propagation of radio waves and detect the presence of interfering signals without the use of test equipment. Even if you are using omnidirectional antennas, radio waves do not really travel the same distance in all directions. Instead, walls, doors, elevator shafts, people, and other obstacles offer varying degrees of attenuation, which causes the radio frequency (RF) radiation pattern to be irregular and unpredictable. As a result, it is often necessary to perform an RF site survey to fully understand the behavior of radio waves within a facility before installing wireless network APs.

Performing a site survey can help you find the right places to set up the APs within your facility, wire them back to the network, and detect potential interference. The steps for performing a preinstallation site survey are as follows:

Step 1 Gather the necessary items.

Step 2 Define the network requirements.

Step 3 Mark up the building diagram.

Step 4 Determine the AP locations.

Step 1: Gather the Necessary Items

You should gather all the items you will need during the site survey:

- **Facility diagram**—Locate a set of building blueprints or diagrams. If none is available, prepare a floor plan drawing that depicts the location of walls, walkways, and so on.

- **AP**—You need to obtain one AP (the test AP)—preferably the exact AP model and similar configuration, such as the same antenna and transmit power levels— that you will use throughout the facility.

- **Extension cord**—You will likely need an extension cord so that you can plug in the AP at different points within your facility, without being limited by the location of electrical outlets.

- **Laptop or PDA**—You need a laptop or PDA so that you can properly test the AP locations you will estimate.

- **Site survey software**—You need to load a wireless LAN site survey tool, such as NetStumbler, onto your mobile device so that you can properly measure RF information to estimate AP locations.

  Many wireless adapters come with their own site survey tools. These should be fine for use during your preinstallation site survey; however, make sure the tool shows channel information, because some do not have this feature.

 NOTE NetStumbler is software that helps network administrators and hotspot owners detect wireless networks and displays details, such as channel, service set identifier (SSID), and signal information. You can use this software to help detect inference from nearby wireless networks and to check the signal strength throughout your facility to ensure proper hotspot coverage. For more information, visit the NetStumbler website at http://www.NetStumbler.com.

Remember that this software is included on the companion CD.

NOTE In addition to NetStumbler, which is free, you can purchase numerous other software programs to help you during the installation and administration of wireless networks.

Although the cost of these tools might not be practical for small or single hotspot locations, the tools really do help when administering large hotspots or multiple hotspot locations or when network performance is very important.

Tools from the following vendors can help during site surveys and when analyzing network issues and RF interference:

■ **AirMagnet**—http://www.airmagnet.com

■ **Ekahau**—http://www.ekahau.com

Step 2: Define the Network Requirements

First you must define the requirements for your hotspot network. Defining these requirements can help later when you are performing the physical site survey testing to ensure that you achieve the amount and quality of coverage you want for your Wi-Fi hotspot.

■ **Coverage areas**—Mark the areas on your facility diagram where you want hotspot coverage within your facility.

■ **Quality of connection**—To find the quality of connection that is best for your situation, think about the number of congruent users and traffic types that you except at your hotspot. You can refer to Table 12-3 for help. After choosing the quality of connection, make note of the recommended signal-to-noise ratio (SNR) in Table 12-3, because you will need this later in the site survey process to ensure good signal coverage.

Table 12-3 *Quality of Connection Definitions*

Quality of Connection	Estimated Congruent Users	Estimated Traffic Type	Recommend SNR (for Use During Testing)
Good	Up to 5	Light use for e-mail, casual browsing, and so on	15 dB or more
Very good	5 or more	Heavy use for downloading, using Internet phones, and so on	25 dB or more

Step 3: Mark Up the Building Diagram

On the building diagram, mark the areas where you want hotspot coverage, and write in the connection quality minimums for each area. Figure 12-10 provides an example.

Figure 12-10 Example of a Marked-Up Building Diagram

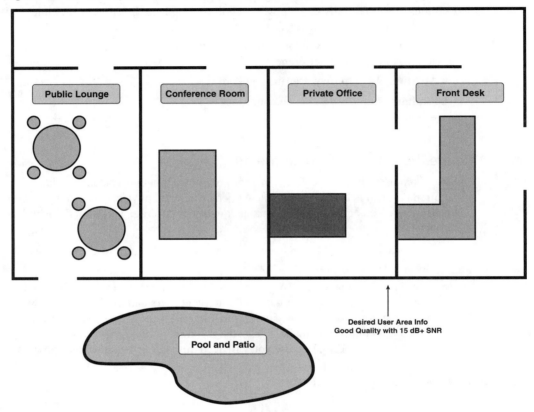

Step 4: Determine the AP Locations

This is where the real site surveying begins. The following sections describe the procedures to follow to accurately determine where to place APs.

Estimate an AP Location

Consider the location of hotspot users and range estimates of the wireless products you are using and the range of any other wireless infrastructure devices (APs, wireless routers, or gateways) in the area. Then pick out a location within your facility that you think would be an ideal spot to place an AP.

Typical indoor AP ranges can vary anywhere between 100 to 300 feet in all directions. Keep in mind that the interior building construction greatly determines the actual ranges you will experience. For example, you would have a much longer range from an AP in a building that was constructed mostly of drywall than a building made of concrete and steel.

In addition, think about the area in which you are placing the AP, such as the number of walls and barriers around. For example, if you are placing an AP in an open space, such as a fairly large waiting room or auditorium, you will likely see a longer range.

Plan for some propagation overlap among adjacent APs, but keep in mind that channel assignments for APs need to be far enough apart to avoid interaccess point interference, as discussed in Appendix A.

Plug in the AP at an Estimated Location

Plug in the test AP at a location, and remember to place the AP in a similar position that it would be in if you were to permanently mount it at that location. Keep in mind that you do not need to provide Internet (or network) access to the AP at this time.

Take Measurements

In these steps, you use your mobile device loaded with a wireless LAN site survey tool, such as NetStumbler, or your wireless adapter tool, and move around the location while monitoring the site survey tool's measurements, particularly the SNR, to ensure that your estimated AP location is good.

NOTE SNR is the difference between the signal and the RF noise at a particular location. This is the best measure you can use to determine an AP's connection quality at a certain location.

As you walk varying distances and directions away from the test AP, check the SNR measurement from the site survey tool. Consider your desired SNR, such as the recommendations in Table 12-3, when determining the AP's range. The recommended SNR value is a minimum level that you should measure. Good signal coverage exists when the SNR is at or above the recommended SNR value. Mark on the diagram the test AP coverage boundary, based on the desired SNR. See Figure 12-11 for an example.

Figure 12-11 Example of Estimated SNR Coverage Boundary of the Test AP

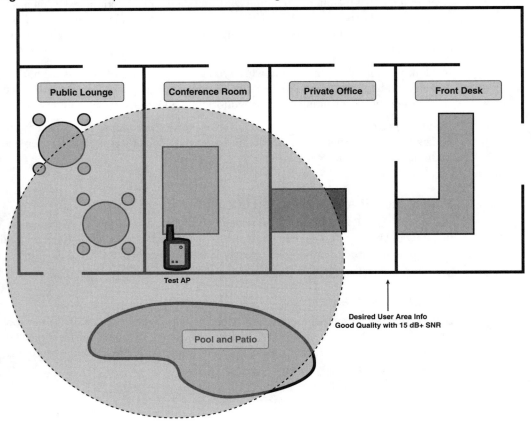

In a multifloor facility, make sure you perform tests and mark boundaries on the floor above and below the test AP, such as those depicted in the next section in Figures 12-12 and 12-13.

Ensure That the Test AP Placement Is Optimum

Ensure that the AP is placed in an optimum location based on the SNR measurements throughout the test AP coverage area. Also consider your desired user areas, any overlapping with other APs, and the power and network connection required.

NOTE   Remember: One AP does not have to cover an entire area. You can colocate multiple APs continuously in a defined area to enable the hotspot coverage of larger areas.

If a certain user area within your facility requires multiple APs to provide adequate coverage, ensure that you have optimum coverage overlap (about 15 percent) with the adjacent APs, or wireless routers and gateways, already measured and noted on the facility diagram. Overlap the coverage of each AP based on your desired SNR, as illustrated in Figures 12-12 and 12-13.

Figure 12-12 Example of Optimum Coverage Overlap: Floor 1

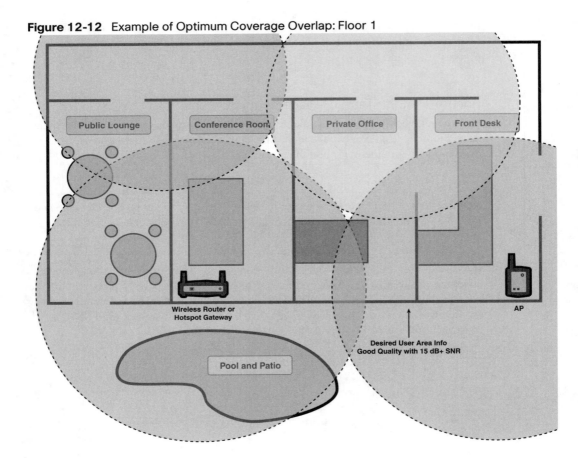

As you see in Figures 12-12 and 12-13, the SNR coverage boundary (based on 15 dBm) of AP 1 just meets up with the wireless gateway SNR coverage boundary (also based on 15 dBm.) However, at the same time, ensure that you will not have excessive overlapping.

Figure 12-13 Example of Optimum Coverage Overlap: Floor 2

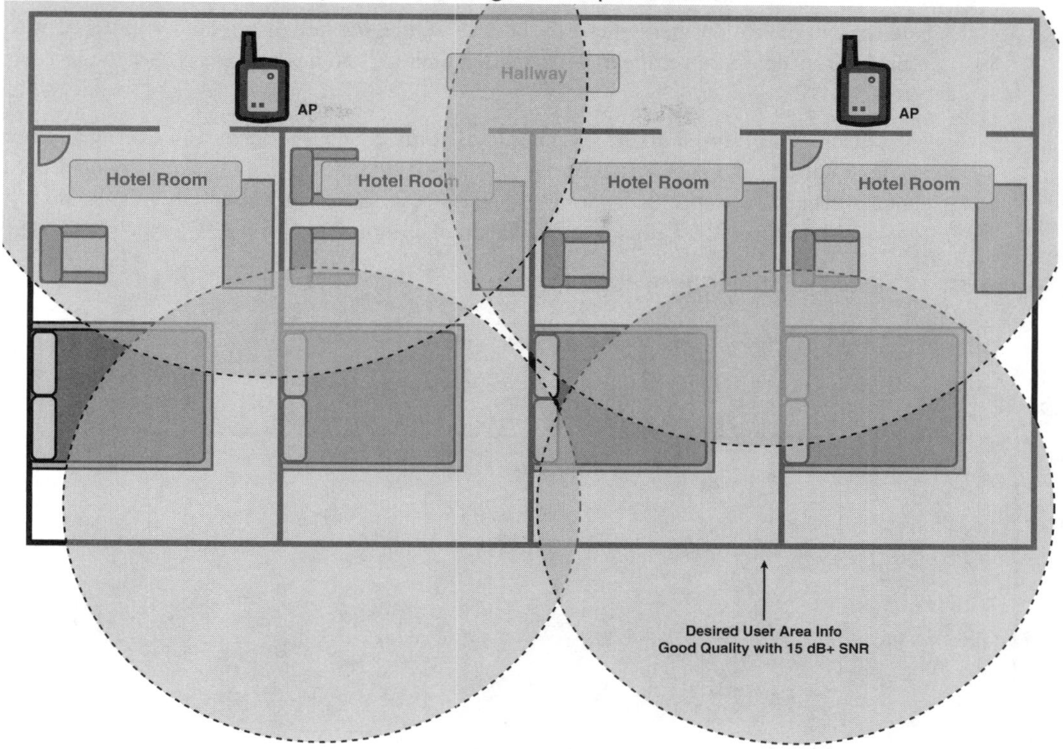

Hallway

AP

Hotel Room   Hotel Room   Hotel Room   Hotel Room

AP

Desired User Area Info
Good Quality with 15 dB+ SNR

After you have planned several AP locations, this requirement will become more difficult. That is because you have to ensure optimum coverage overlap with all the adjacent APs:

- **If the test AP location is good**—Double-check that you have marked, on the diagram, the SNR coverage boundary of the test AP. In addition, make note of any electrical outlets and any noticeable routes to run Ethernet cabling to provide power or a network (Internet) connection to the AP.

   Repeat these steps until you have achieved the desired coverage as noted on the facility diagram.

- **If the test AP location is not good**—Based on the SNR measurements you have seen around the test AP location, move the AP and repeat the steps to find an optimum AP location.

Assign AP Channels

After you have identified where all the APs will be located throughout your facility, to provide sufficient coverage in your desired area(s), you must properly assign channels to each AP.

As discussed in Appendix A, you should use only channels 1, 6, and 11 among all your APs. In addition, make sure the coverage of APs that are set on the same channel does not overlap. Overlapping causes interaccess point interference, which you should try to avoid. Figure 12-14 illustrates AP channel assignment.

Figure 12-14 Example of AP Channel Assignment on the Building Diagram

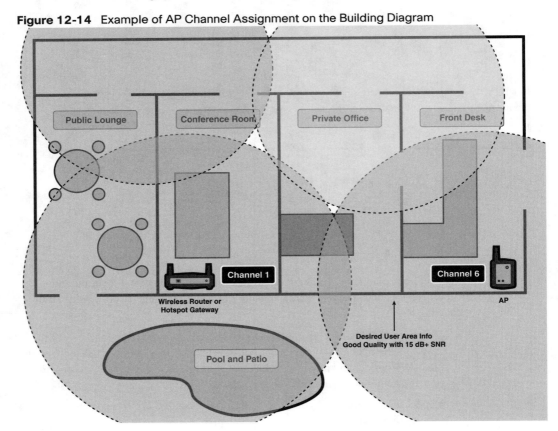

Figure 12-14 Example of AP Channel Assignment on the Building Diagram

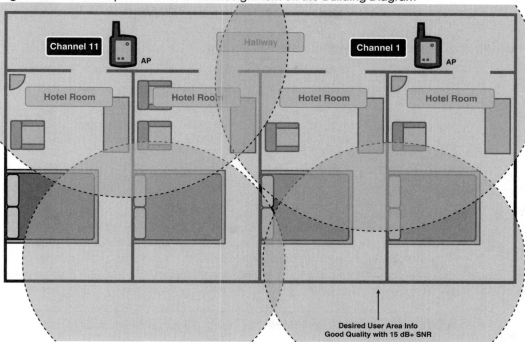

 NOTE Check for existing wireless networks before assigning channels for your APs. Make sure you account for these other wireless networks to avoid interaccess point interference.

Make sure you write the channel assignments on the building diagram for each AP. Also, number the AP locations to make the later installation easier.

Network and Power Connection Options

You can connect the APs, which will be mounted throughout your facility, to the network in a few ways to receive Internet access and a power source. The preferred network connection method is Ethernet cable, because it provides the highest-quality connection. In addition, you can use Ethernet cabling to provide a power source to your APs, instead of plugging them into an outlet or running new electrical lines. This technology is called *power over Ethernet* (PoE).

If running Ethernet cabling through the facility is not feasible, you can use existing electrical outlets for your network connection. See Table 12-4 to help figure out which method to use.

Table 12-4 *Comparison of Network Connection Options*

Method	Typical Data Rate	Price	Maximum Distance
Electrical wiring	14 Mbps	$40–$60 per bridge	200–300 meters (or 656–984 feet)
Ethernet cabling	10 or 100 Mbps	$5–$15 for 50 to 100 feet	100 to 350 meters (or 328-1148 feet)

Power Lines

With proper adapters or bridges, you can use the existing electrical wiring of a facility to send and receive network data, as depicted in Figure 12-15. This provides many places where you can plug APs into the network, eliminating the need to run new Ethernet cabling throughout the facility. HomePlug is the leading industry alliance that provides certification for power line networking devices.

NOTE An easy way to find HomePlug-certified power line devices is to refer to their website at http://www.homeplug.org.

HomePlug-certified devices have a typical data rate of up to 14 Mbps. That is much lower than Ethernet cabling, which can typically support 100 Mbps or higher. However, the speed of HomePlug is still much greater than common Internet speeds, which range from 300 kbps to 4 Mbps. Therefore, using power line networking devices provides a feasible alterative to installing and using Ethernet cables to provide a network or Internet connection around your facility to plug in APs.

Bear in mind that power line networking devices typically need to be within 200 to 300 meters (or 656 to 984 feet) of each other and within the same phase of the electrical distribution system (or on the same electrical lines) to work properly. Before getting too far with your hotspot installation, you should test a pair of power line bridges to confirm that they will connect to each other and work as intended.

Power line networking devices generally use 56-bit Data Encryption Standard (DES) to help prevent people from plugging into your electrical system to eavesdrop. They also typically have a built-in surge protector. These devices might be affected by other components that are plugged into the electrical system, such as hairdryers, electric drills/saws, vacuum cleaners, and window-mounted air conditioners.

Figure 12-15 Example of a Power Line Network Providing Network Connection for APs

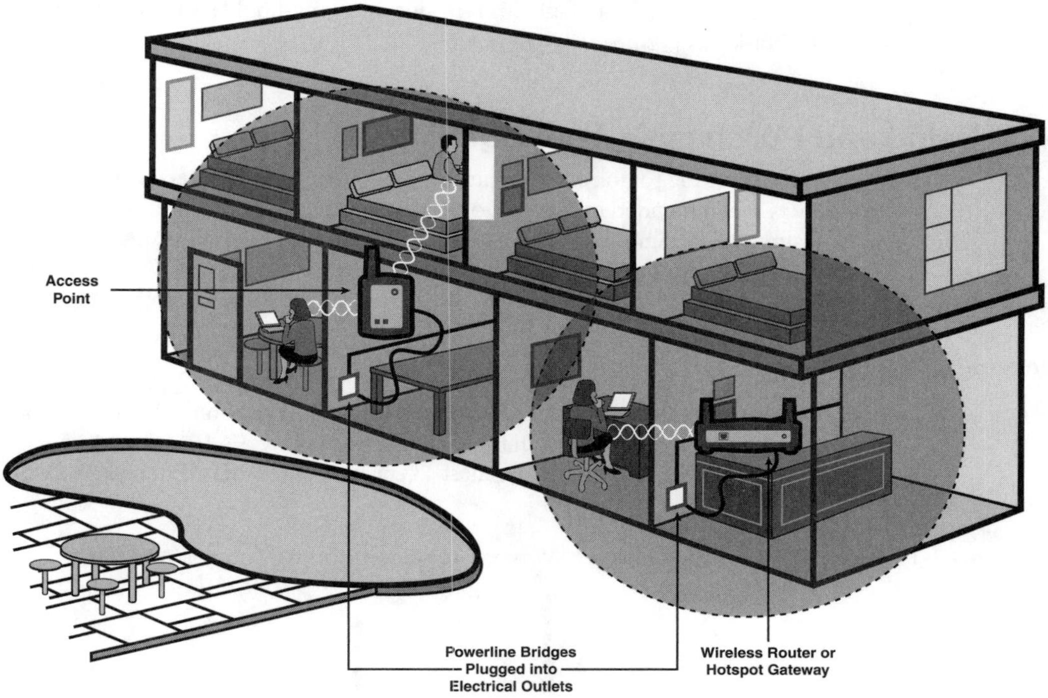

Access Point

Powerline Bridges
Plugged into
Electrical Outlets

Wireless Router or
Hotspot Gateway

Running Ethernet Cable

As mentioned earlier, the use of Ethernet cable is the preferred method to provide APs with a network connection.

A few different types of Ethernet cabling exist. Your best bet is to use unshielded twisted-pair (UTP) Category 5 enhanced (CAT5e) Ethernet cabling. In addition, you can choose from two different types:

- **Stranded**—Stranded cable has several small-gauge wires in each insulation sleeve, making it more flexible and more suitable for shorter distances, such as 30 feet or less.

- **Solid**—Solid cable has one larger-gauge wire in each sleeve, thus providing better electrical performance than stranded cable. This cabling is traditionally used for permanent installations, such as inside walls and through ceilings. This is also the recommended cabling to provide network connections to your APs throughout your facility. However, keep in mind that this cabling is not as flexible. You need to take proper care of it as recommended by the manufacturer or retailer. When dealing with this type of cable, you should try not to create sharp bends or kinks.

Choosing and Purchasing Your Equipment

When you are looking for the equipment for your AP expansion project, consider using the products recommended in this section. These products are not usually available at local consumer electronics stores. Try purchasing them on Internet stores such as Amazon.com or Buy.com.

Access Points

Make sure you order the correct number of APs for your expansion, which you should know after completing the preinstallation site survey. Figure 12-16 shows the recommended AP that you should purchase. Typical cost for this AP ranges from $60 to $80.

Figure 12-16   Recommended AP: Linksys Wireless-G Access Point (Model # WAP54G)

Power Line Devices

If you will use this method to provide the network connections for your APs, use the information from your site survey. Take some time to carefully examine your facility to determine which and how many power line devices you need based on the power line manufacturer or vendor installation guides so that you can give each AP a network connection. You likely need one bridge to connect the Internet to your power line network and a bridge for each AP.

For more information about HomePlug-certified power line devices, refer to their website at http://www.homeplug.org.

Figure 12-17 shows the recommended power line bridge that you should purchase. Typical cost for this device ranges from $50 to $100.

Figure 12-17 Recommended Power Line Bridge: Linksys Instant Power Line EtherFast 10/100 Bridge (Model #PLEBR10)

Ethernet Cable

If you will use this method to provide the network connections for your APs, use the information from your site survey and devote some time to carefully examining your facility to determine how many Ethernet cables you need and of what lengths. Make sure you order prefabricated or custom cabling unless you want to take on the task of wiring connectors yourself, which is difficult for someone who has not done that before.

You can order Ethernet cabling at online stores such as these:

http://www.cat5ecableguy.com
http://www.ramelectronics.net
http://www.lanshack.com

PoE

If you will use this method to provide power to your APs rather than plugging into regular electrical outlets, use the information from your site survey. Devote some time to carefully examining your facility to determine which and how many PoE devices you need based on the PoE manufacturer or vendor installation guides so that you can give each AP a combined power and network connection.

Figure 12-18 shows the recommended PoE adapter kit that you should purchase. Typical cost for this device ranges from $35 to $70.

Figure 12-18 Recommended PoE Adapter Kit: Linksys 12-Volt PoE Adapter Kit
(Model #WAPPOE12)

Configuring the APs

Before installing APs throughout your facility, configure them at a staging area. You can begin by assigning the location numbers to each AP with a permanent marker, sticky note, and so on so that you can properly configure the channel assignments.

- **Same SSID**—You should set the same SSID for all the APs that will be a part of your wireless network or Wi-Fi hotspot. This allows users to roam seamlessly over your entire hotspot network.

- **Assignment of proper channels**—Be sure to set the channels based on the assignments you made during the site survey and the numbers attached to or written on the APs.

- **AP isolation**—Although this feature is not common in all APs, when enabled, it provides some extra security to the hotspot users. It works by isolating users from each other and prevents people from accessing each other's shared files.

  You usually find this feature in the advanced wireless settings. You can usually turn it on and off.

Physical Installation

You are almost finished! Now you can begin with the physical installation of your APs.

- **Install network and power connections**—You should install your network and power connections, such as Ethernet cabling or power line devices. Be sure to consult the installation guides.

- **Mount APs**—Securely mount your APs to ensure that the general public cannot get their hands on them. Good mounting locations might be high on the wall or ceiling or above a drop-down ceiling.

- **Connect the network and power cables**—After your network and power connections are in place and the APs are mounted, all you should have to do is connect the cables.

Chapter Review

This chapter discussed ways to increase the coverage area of your Wi-Fi hotspot.

Make sure you keep in mind the following:

- You can use higher-gain antennas.
  - Easy
  - Inexpensive
  - Slight increase in coverage
- You can use wireless repeaters.
  - Fairly challenging
  - Moderately expensive
  - Allows you to expand your hotspot network without the use of Ethernet cabling
- You can add APs.
  - Can be challenging
  - Moderately expensive
  - Allows you to expand your hotspot network virtually as big as you want, but it takes quite a bit of time and effort

Chapter 13

Using Wi-Fi Networks

If you are not familiar with using Wi-Fi networks, this chapter can help you a great deal. Along with other functions you need to know when using your hotspot or other wireless networks, this chapter discusses how to use the Windows XP Wireless Zero Configuration tool. This also helps prepare you for assisting your hotspot users.

NOTE   Recommended practice is to use at least the Windows XP operating system when using wireless networks because of the built-in networking tools. If you are currently using an older operating system, such as Windows 98 or Windows Me, upgrade to the latest version. This gives you a much better experience when using wireless networks. Therefore, this chapter gives instructions only for Windows XP.

Keeping Your Operating System Up-to-Date

Keep in mind that when using wireless or wired networks, you should always keep your operating system up-to-date with the latest service packs and updates. This helps plug any known security holes in the operating system and makes your experience safer. In addition, Windows XP users should download updates so that the Wireless Zero Configuration utility supports the current technologies.

Download Windows operating system updates online at http://windowsupdate.microsoft.com/.

Enabling and Disabling Your Network Adapter

You should disconnect or disable your network adapter when you are not using your network. For security reasons, this is especially true when you are using unsecured wireless networks such as hotspots. Doing so also helps save battery power when you are using laptops and other mobile devices. In addition, knowing how to disable and enable your network adapter might help when you are troubleshooting problems.

Using the Start Menu

You can turn your network adapter on and off via the Start menu:

Step 1   In the lower-left corner of Windows, click the **Start** button.

Step 2   Hover the mouse pointer over the **Connect To** option, as shown in Figure 13-1.

Figure 13-1   Hovering over the Connect To Option

If this option is not available, your Start menu is likely in Classic mode. In that case, hover over the **Settings** option, and then hover over the **Network Connections** option.

Step 3   To enable a wireless connection, click it.

Step 4   To disable a wireless connection, right-click it and click the **Disable** option.

Using the System Tray

An easier and quicker way to disable your network adapter is via the system tray using the following steps:

Step 1   Right-click the system tray icon of the wireless adapter.

Step 2   Click the **Disable** option, as shown in Figure 13-2.

Figure 13-2   Disabling Your Wireless Network Adapter

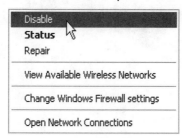

Toggling Between Windows XP and the Manufacturer Utility

If you have not noticed yet, Windows XP has a built-in wireless configuration utility. In addition, most wireless adapters have a custom wireless configuration utility that you can use. Usually you can pick which utility you want to use.

Most wireless vendors automatically set up their utility to work. Therefore, if you want to use their utility, you should not have to make changes to get their utility working. However, if you disabled it earlier or if it is not working, try disabling the Windows XP utility and stopping the Wireless Zero Configuration Service, using the instructions in this section.

On the other hand, if you want to use the Windows XP configuration utility, called the *Wireless Zero Configuration*, instead of the vendor's configuration utility, you probably need to do some things to enable it. First try enabling the Windows XP utility using the instructions described in the following sections.

Enabling/Disabling the Windows XP Utility

You can switch between the Windows XP and the manufacturer's utility by following these steps:

Step 1   In the lower-left corner of Windows, click the **Start** button.

Step 2   Hover the mouse pointer over the **Connect To** option, as shown in Figure 13-3.

Figure 13-3   Hovering over the Connect To Option

If the **Connect To** option is not available, your Start menu is likely in classic mode. In that case, hover over the **Settings** option, and then hover over the **Network Connections** option.

Step 3   Right-click the wireless adapter, and click the **Properties** option.

Step 4   Click the tab labeled **Wireless Networks**.

Step 5   If you do not see the Wireless Networks tab, make sure that the wireless adapter is enabled. In addition, the Wireless Zero Configuration service might be disabled; therefore, you might want to follow the instructions in the next section and then continue with this step.

Step 6   As needed, check or uncheck the option **Use Windows to configure my wireless network settings**, as shown in Figure 13-4.

Figure 13-4   Enabling/Disabling the Windows XP Utility

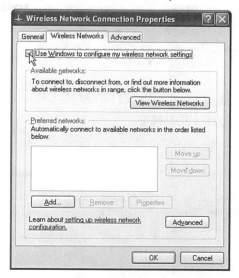

Step 7   Click **OK** to apply the changes.

Starting/Stopping the Wireless Zero Configuration Service

Start and stop the Wireless Zero Configuration service that is used to run the Windows XP configuration utility by doing the following:

Step 1   In the lower-left corner of Windows, click the **Start** button.

Step 2   Click **Run**.

Step 3   Enter **%SystemRoot%\system32\services.msc /s**, as shown in Figure 13-5, and then click **OK**.

Figure 13-5   Accessing Windows Services Control Panel

Step 4   Scroll down to the **Wireless Zero Configuration** listing, and double-click it.

Step 5 To enable, click the **Start** button. In the **Startup type** drop-down list, select **Automatic**, and then click **Apply**.

Step 6 To disable, click the **Stop** button. In the **Startup type** drop-down list, select **Disabled**, and then click **Apply**.

Connecting to a Wi-Fi Network Using the Windows XP Configuration Utility

One of the first things you should know is how to connect to wireless networks because you must do so before you can access the Internet via your network. To connect to a wireless network using the Windows XP Configuration utility, do the following:

Step 1 Right-click the wireless adapter system tray icon and click the **View Available Wireless Networks** option, as shown in Figure 13-6.

Figure 13-6   Clicking the View Available Wireless Networks Option

Step 2 Click the desired wireless network.

Step 3 Click the **Connect** button, as shown in Figure 13-7.

Step 4 If the wireless network is not using an encryption method, you need to verify that you understand the consequences of connecting to an unsecured network, such as a hotspot, by clicking the **Connect Anyway** button in the popup window.

Step 5 If the wireless network is using encryption, you need to input the network key in the popup window and click **Connect.**

Figure 13-7   Clicking the Connect Option

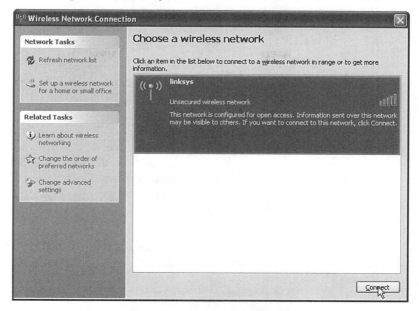

Checking the Connection Status

You can easily check the connection status of your wireless adapter. This status information can help when you are troubleshooting connection problems.

Using the System Tray

To quickly see the status of your connection, follow these steps:

Step 1   Hover over the wireless adapter system tray icon.

Step 2   You should see the status information popup, as shown in Figure 13-8. If you are connected to a network, the popup shows the network name (Service Set Identifier, or SSID) you are connected to, the speed (or data rate), and the signal strength of the connection.

Figure 13-8   Hovering over the System Tray Icon

Using the Status Window

To view details of your connection, follow these steps:

Step 1 Double-click the wireless adapter system tray icon.

Step 2 As shown in Figure 13-9, you should see the connection and activity status. This lets you know the network name (SSID) you are connected to, how long you have been connected, the speed (or data rate), and the signal strength of the connection. You can also see how many packets have been sent and received while you have been connected.

If both the wireless network adapter you are using and the wireless router or access point are 802.11g-compliant, the best possible data rate would be 54 Mbps. When you are using products with a speed-booster feature, the data rate might be higher. If the network devices, however, support only 802.11b, the highest data rate possible is 11 Mbps.

In addition, this window gives you another way to disable your network adapter, go to the properties of the adapter, and go to the View Available Wireless Networks window.

Figure 13-9 Wireless Network Connection General Status

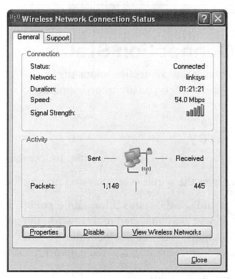

Step 3 Click the **Support** tab.

As Figure 13-10 illustrates, you should see the current IP address information of your wireless adapter.

Figure 13-10 Wireless Network Connection Support Status

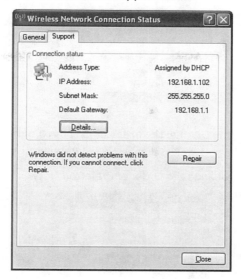

Clearly shown in Figure 13-10 is the address type, or the way the IP address was received, the IP address assigned to your computer, the subnet mask, and the default gateway, which is the IP address of the device you are connected through, such as a wireless router.

Editing Your Preferred Network List

The preferred network list is a prioritized list of networks you would like to connect to. You can add networks to the list, which saves time, especially when you are using encrypted wireless networks. Your wireless adapter automatically connects to networks in the preferred list, which avoids the need to enter encryption keys on secure networks.

Accessing the Preferred Network List

Follow these steps to get to the preferred network list:

Step 1 Right-click the wireless adapter system tray icon, and click the **View Available Wireless Networks** option, as shown in Figure 13-11.

Figure 13-11 Clicking the View Available Wireless Networks Option

> **Step 2** Click the **Change the order of preferred networks** option, in the Related Tasks selection, as shown in Figure 13-12.

Figure 13-12 Clicking the Change the Order of Preferred Networks Option

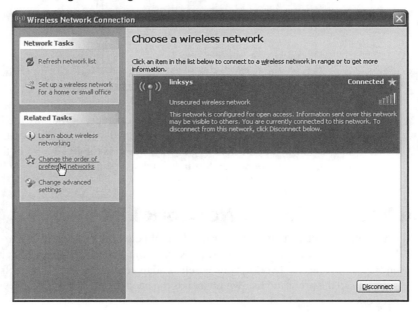

Changing the Preferred Order

You can move the order of your wireless networks by selecting a network and clicking the **Move up** or **Move down** buttons, as shown in Figure 13-13.

Figure 13-13 Changing the Priority of a Preferred Network

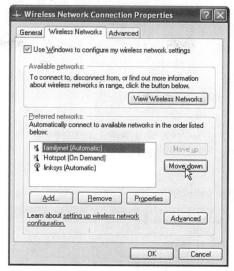

Adding a Preferred Network

If you need to add a network to the preferred list, do so by following these steps:

Step 1 Click the **Add** button.

Step 2 Enter the applicable information about the wireless network you want to add to your preferred list. See Figure 13-14 for an example.

Figure 13-14 Wireless Network Properties

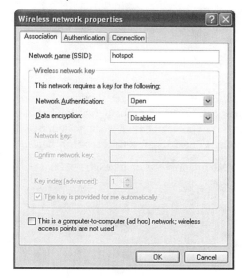

Step 3   If the network does not have encryption enabled, such as might be the case with public hotspots, select **Open** authentication, and set data encryption to **Disabled**.

Step 4   If you are trying to add an ad-hoc or peer-to-peer network to your preferred list, mark the appropriate check box on the bottom of the window. With hotspots, you do not choose ad-hoc or peer-to-peer. These types of networks allow wireless computers to communicate directly with each other without a wireless router or access point.

Step 5   Select the **Authentication** tab, as shown in Figure 13-15, and make any necessary changes. Most likely you will not need to with a hotspot.

Figure 13-15   Authentication Settings of the Wireless Network

Step 6   Select the **Connection** tab, as shown in Figure 13-16. If you want to automatically connect to the network when it is available, mark the check box. This is not always suggested. See the Caution and Note following Figure 13-16 for more information.

Step 7   Click **OK** to apply the changes.

Figure 13-16 Connection Settings of the Wireless Network

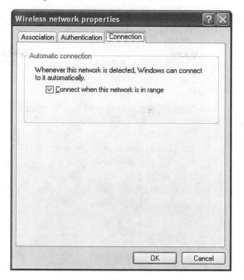

NOTE If you add a preferred ad-hoc or peer-to-peer network to your preferred list, and either it is higher priority than other networks on the list or no other *preferred* networks are nearby, the wireless adapter automatically starts accepting other nearby ad-hoc clients based on the ad-hoc network information that you added to the preferred list. Therefore, others can freely connect to the ad-hoc network and view any shared files on your computer. If the peer-to-peer network you added has encryption enabled, other users need to know the network key to connect. However, for better security, you should not set the network to automatically connect when available. For more information, see Step 4 in the preceding list.

CAUTION Remember that when you are setting a preferred network to automatically connect when available, it basically connects to any network with that same network name (or SSID). Therefore, you should not set to automatically connect to networks with common or default names, such as "default" and "linksys."

Advanced Options

Review and make any applicable changes to the Advanced options:

Step 1 Click the **Advanced** button.

Step 2 Make any desired changes. See Figure 13-17 for an example.

Figure 13-17 Advanced Settings

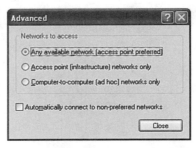

Step 3 Remember that infrastructure networks are those with wireless routers or access points, such as hotspot networks.

Step 4 The **Any available network (access point preferred)** option is usually recommended. It automatically connects only to access points and computer-to-computer networks that are listed in your preferred list.

Step 5 If you want to automatically connect to any available wireless network when it becomes available, mark the appropriate check box. For security reasons, this is not recommended, because you will automatically be connected to networks even if they are not in your preferred list.

Step 6 Click **Close** to apply the changes.

Sharing Files

One of the benefits of using wireless or wired networks is the ability to share files among the network users. Enabling sharing on hotspots and other networks that are not secured by encryption is not suggested. However, on private networks, it comes in handy. First, you must enable sharing on certain folders, or move files to your Windows XP Shared Documents folder. Then you should be able to access the folders on other computers that are connected to the same network.

Enabling Shared Folders

Windows XP, by default, has a folder called **Shared Documents** under **My Computer**, with sharing enabled. To quickly share files with other network users, you can copy or drag files into this folder. You can also enable sharing of other folders, as documented in the following steps:

Step 1 Double-click **My Computer** on your desktop.

Step 2 Browse to the folder you would like to share, right-click the folder, and click the **Sharing and Security** option, as shown in Figure 13-18.

Figure 13-18 Clicking the Sharing and Security Option

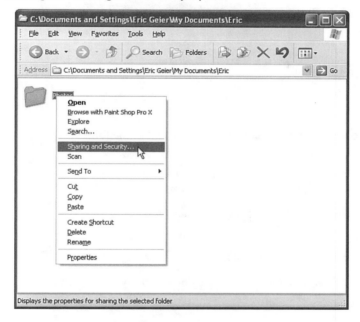

Step 3 Check the **Share this folder on the network** option, as shown in Figure 13-19.

Figure 13-19 Clicking the Share This Folder on the Network Option

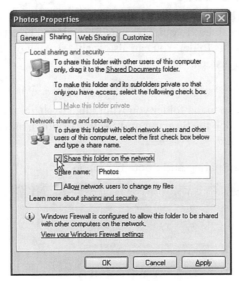

Step 4 Specify a share name that describes the folder or files you are sharing.

Step 5 Check the **Allow network users to change my files** option if you want to give other network users this privilege.

Step 6 Click **OK** to apply the changes.

Accessing Shared Folders

You can access the shared folders on your network using these steps:

Step 1 Double-click **My Network Places** on your desktop.

Step 2 Click the **View workgroup computers** option under Network Tasks, as shown in Figure 13-20. To browse computers within other workgroups, click the **Up** button; then double-click the desired workgroup.

Step 3 Double-click the computer you want to browse, as shown in Figure 13-21.

Step 4 Double-click the desired shared folder.

Figure 13-20 Clicking the View Workgroup Computers Option

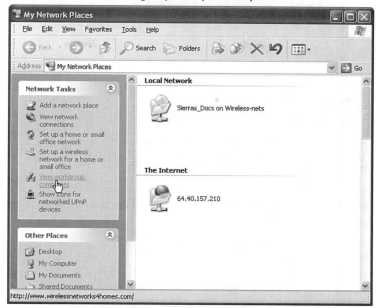

Figure 13-21 Clicking a Computer Network Shortcut

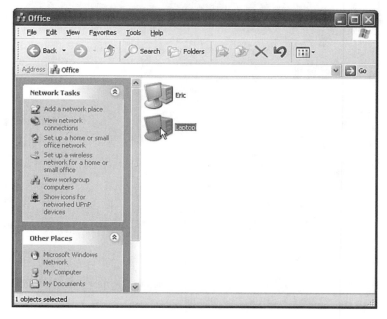

Sharing Printers

One of the ways to share printers on a network is to connect a printer directly to a computer within the network and set it up to be shared in Windows. This is the method discussed in the following sections.

Enabling Shared Printers

First you must enable the sharing of the printer among the network:

Step 1 In the lower-left corner of Windows, click the **Start** button.

Step 2 Click **Printers and Faxes**.

Step 3 If this option is not available, your Start menu is likely in Classic mode. Therefore, hover over the **Settings** option and click **Printers and Faxes**.

Step 4 Right-click the printer you would like to share, and click **Sharing**, as shown in Figure 13-22.

Figure 13-22 Clicking the Sharing Option

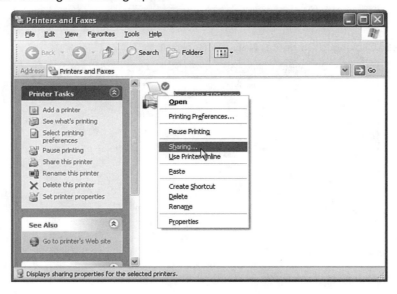

Step 5 Mark the **Share this printer** option.

Step 6 Specify a share name that describes the printer you are sharing. See Figure 13-23 for an example.

Figure 13-23 Specifying a Share Name for the Printer

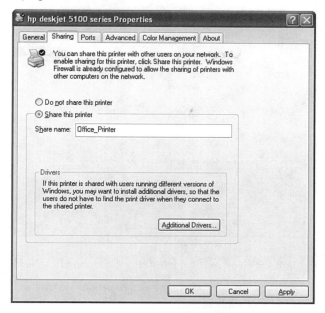

Step 7   Click **OK** to apply the changes.

Adding Shared Printers to Computers

Now you can set up or add a shared network printer on a specific computer:

Step 1   In the lower-left corner of Windows, click the **Start** button.

Step 2   Click **Printers and Faxes**.

Step 3   If this option is not available, your Start menu is likely in Classic mode. In that case, hover over the **Settings** option and click **Printers and Faxes**.

Step 4   Under the **File** menu, click **Add Printer**. When the wizard starts, click **Next**.

Step 5   Click the **A network printer, or a printer attached to another computer** option, as shown in Figure 13-24, and click **Next**.

Figure 13-24 Clicking the Network Printer Option

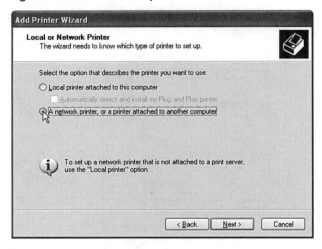

Step 6 Mark the **Browse for a printer** option, and click **Next**.

Step 7 Find the computer where the shared printer is attached, double-click it, and then click **Next**.

Step 8 Click the shared printer you would like to set up, as shown in Figure 13-25, and click **Next**.

Figure 13-25 Clicking the Desired Shared Printer

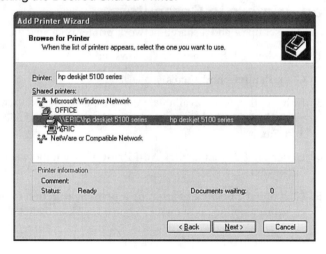

Step 9 Specify whether you want to set this shared printer to the default printer, and then click **Next**.

Step 10 Make sure the information is correct, and click **Finish**.

Chapter Summary

You have been introduced to the main tasks you need to know when using Wi-Fi networks. Now you are better equipped when using your new Wi-Fi hotspot or any other wireless network to which you might have access, such as in your home or office. Keep in mind a few main points, covered in this chapter:

- Keep your operating system up-to-date.

- Disable your network adapter(s) when you are not using it.

- Indicate whether you want to use Windows XP to configure your wireless network settings when you are toggling between Windows XP and the manufacturer's utility.

- When you want to use the Windows XP configuration utility, you must have the Zero Configuration Service enabled.

- Use the preferred wireless network list to streamline your Wi-Fi experiences.

Part IV: **Appendix**

Appendix A   Understanding Wi-Fi Signals

Appendix A

Understanding Wi-Fi Signals

Learning more about wireless, such as the mechanics of Wi-Fi networks and challenges of radio frequency (RF) interference, can help you during the installation and administration of your Wi-Fi hotspot.

Comparing 802.11 Standards

As mentioned in Chapter 1, "The Basics of Wi-Fi Hotspots," Wi-Fi networks use a technology that is specified within a standard called *802.11*. The standard is basically written documents formed by members of the IEEE. These documents help manufacturers develop wireless products so that they will work together with wireless devices from every vendor that follows the standard.

802.11 comes in several versions that have different characteristics, as shown in Table A-1.

Table A-1   *Comparison of 802.11 Standards*

Standard	Frequency	Maximum Data Rate	Average Line-of-Sight Range	Compatibility
802.11b	2.4 GHz	11 Mbps	300 ft	Interoperable with 802.11g
802.11g	2.4 GHz	54 Mbps	300 ft	Interoperable with 802.11b
802.11a	5 GHz	54 Mbps	225 ft	Not interoperable with 802.11b or 802.11g
802.11n	2.4 GHz	540 Mbps	—	Interoperable with 802.11b/g

NOTE   It is a frequently misunderstood belief that the actual traffic on a wireless network travels at the maximum or "raw" data rate, such as shown in Table A-1.

The actual data rates that users will experience will be much less, up to 50 percent less, due to the normal overhead of the network protocol.

The most widely used standard today is 802.11g, which is similar to 802.11b. However, 802.11g can handle a much greater data rate, up to 54 Mbps. The 802.11g standard is an improved version of 802.11b, in which the main upgrade is the higher data rates, or speeds. The 802.11g standard was created to be backward-compatible with 802.11b. Therefore, it is possible to mix 802.11b and 802.11g devices within the same wireless network. The 802.11a standard, though, is not compatible with these two standards and does not even use the same frequency band.

A drawback to using the 802.11b and 802.11g standards is that they both use the 2.4-GHz frequency band, which has more potential congestion. Other devices such as cordless phones, wireless speakers and headphones, and baby monitors use this band. Microwave ovens also emit radio waves in this range and can cause interference. However, these two standards are most likely the best choice for use in public hotspots because nearly all client devices today implement 802.11g. The 802.11a standard is not widely used throughout the consumer market.

802.11n is an evolving wireless networking standard used for Wi-Fi devices. This upcoming standard plans to use the 2.4-GHz frequency band, as do 802.11b and g, with data rates up to 540 Mbps, which is 10 times faster than existing standards. In addition, these products will have a much longer range by using a powerful smart-antenna technology, called *Multiple Input Multiple Output* (MIMO), which is already available in some wireless networking products.

Wireless networking vendors have already started selling products based on this technology. The products are referred to as *pre-n* or *802.11n draft* products. With these prestandard components, the user adapter and your AP (or router) must be manufactured by the same vendor.

In addition, even with finalized 802.11n products, both the AP, or wireless router, and the user's wireless adapter have to be 802.11n to achieve all the benefits. Even though it might take a few years for the majority of Wi-Fi users to upgrade, implementing 802.11n (when finalized) for your Wi-Fi hotspot might not be a bad idea, because 802.11b/g users might still receive benefits such as a slight increase in range.

 NOTE   Keep in mind that even though 802.11n might increase tenfold the data rate or speed of a wireless network, typical Internet connection speeds are much lower, such as 3 or 4 Mbps or lower. Therefore, even if the network operates at 540 Mbps, users who are just browsing the web and sending e-mail, such as at hotspots, do not see much of a speed advantage when using 802.11n. However, file sharing between computers on the same private network is much faster for 802.11n users.

Wi-Fi System Operation

All 802.11 technologies operate in the same manner. The operational functions, such as connecting, scanning, and roaming between APs, are controlled by the MAC layer, which is specified in the 802.11 standard. This section covers how the main MAC operations of wireless networks work.

Beacons

Access points (APs) and wireless routers broadcast beacons via the airwaves, as shown in Figure A-1. The beacons provide a means of identifying APs and wireless routers to wireless clients. These beacons also contain pertinent information about the wireless network to inform nearby wireless clients of the network and to synchronize the wireless clients that are already part of the network.

Figure A-1 Example of Beacon Broadcasts

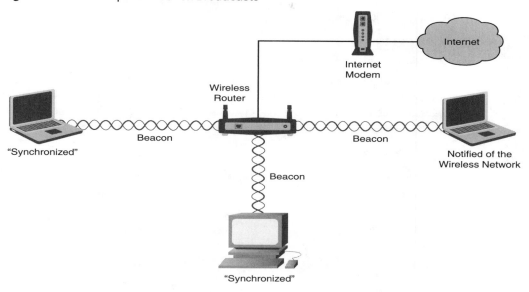

Beacons are sent periodically, starting as soon as you plug in the AP or wireless router, at an interval of 1 to 65,535 milliseconds. The default interval that most vendors use is 100 milliseconds, which equates to 10 beacons being sent every second. For hotspot installations, leave the beacon interval set to 100 milliseconds.

NOTE Most APs and wireless routers allow you to disable service set identifier (SSID) broadcasting, which removes the SSID from beacons. This helps hide the network from others. Obviously, you would not want to disable SSID broadcasting on your hotspot network; however, this feature might be useful if you have a separate private network.

The beacons contain information, such as the SSID (name) of the network, supported data rates, timestamp, and more about the wireless network. The wireless client uses this information to determine which AP or wireless router to connect to.

Wireless Client Scanning

Wireless clients (or radio cards) are constantly listening for activity in their specific frequency band. Wireless clients have two main methods to scan for wireless networks (APs and wireless routers):

- Active scanning
- Passive scanning

Active scanning is used when a wireless client wants to search for a specific wireless network. The wireless client is depicted in Figure A-2. It sends a packet, called a *probe request*, on each channel, asking if a network, or an AP/wireless router, is nearby. The wireless client can ask either for a specific network or for any wireless network.

Figure A-2   Example of a Wireless Client Actively Scanning

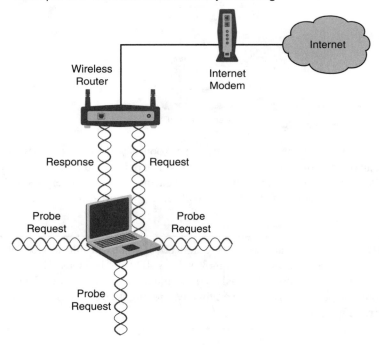

If the wireless client is probing for a specific network, only networks that match the SSID in the request respond with a probe response. However, if the wireless client is probing for any wireless networks nearby, all the APs or wireless routers that "hear" the request respond with a probe response.

Passive scanning, by contrast, takes a hands-off approach. In this case, the wireless client just listens for beacons on each channel. Most wireless clients use a combination of active and passive scanning using proprietary mechanisms. Even when a wireless client is connected to a wireless network, it still periodically scans other channels for nearby wireless networks. This is necessary if the user is roaming through a facility to determine whether to connect to a different AP or wireless router. With both scanning methods, the wireless client stores the information from the wireless networks it discovers. Client software, such as Windows XP, displays a list of applicable wireless networks to the user.

Connecting

Wireless clients have a special sequence they go through each time they want to initiate a connection with a wireless network. The sequence is started when the wireless client is given instructions to initiate a connection with a particular wireless network, from software such as Windows XP or the vendor configuration utility within the computer. For example, the person who is using the computer can view a list of available networks and click a button to connect to a particular network. This initiates the connection process with the applicable network.

Sending and Receiving

In infrastructure wireless networks, such as hotspots, the APs or wireless routers are the coordinators that regulate the traffic from the wireless clients. A common misconception is that the wireless clients send and receive traffic directly to and from each other. However, as shown in Figure A-3, all the traffic goes through the AP, even if a wireless client is accessing or transferring shared files from another wireless client on the network. Figure A-4 depicts the traffic flow when a wireless client is accessing the Internet.

Figure A-3   Example of Transferring a File Within a Wireless Network

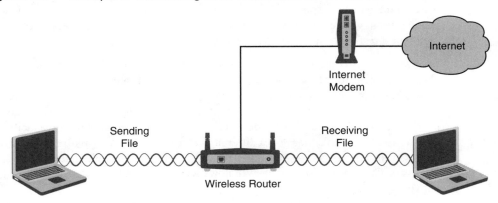

Figure A-4   Example of a Wireless Client Communicating with the Internet

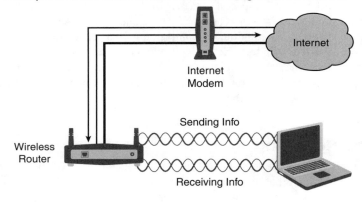

Nonoverlapping Channels

The two widely used wireless networking standards (802.11b and g) operate in the 2.4-GHz frequency band. The total RF allocated space for transmissions is approximately 72 MHz. In this total allocated RF space, 14 defined channels exist.

NOTE Although 14 channels exist overall, only 11 of them are legal for use in the United States. However, in Japan, all 14 channels are available. Countries in Europe and most of the rest of the world can use channels 1 through 13.

When a wireless client or AP sends something, it transmits signals on a channel (1 through 14) that occupies about 22 MHz out of the 72 MHz total allocated space. Simple math (14 channels × 22 MHz) shows that at least 308 MHz of RF space is needed to accommodate 14 channels. However, only 72 MHz of space exists for all the channels, and the frequencies that the channels use overlap. Theoretically, not enough RF space is available for each channel to be active at the same time, at least without the potential for problems.

Therefore, as illustrated in Figure A-5, all but three channels overlap each other. Keep in mind that the figure shows only channels 1 through 11, which are legal for use in the United States.

Figure A-5   DSSS Channels

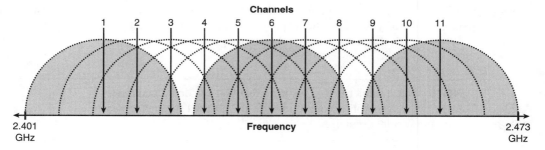

This is why you should use only the nonoverlapping channels (1, 6, and 11) if you are implementing more than one AP or wireless router in your hotspot. The use of a different nonoverlapping channel for adjacent APs and routers improves performance by reducing interference. Figure A-6 illustrates an example of how you can assign the channels of your APs. Even though the wireless coverage of the APs (called *radio cells*) might overlap, you should not have a problem if the nonoverlapping channels are utilized.

Figure A-6   Example of Using Nonoverlapping Channels

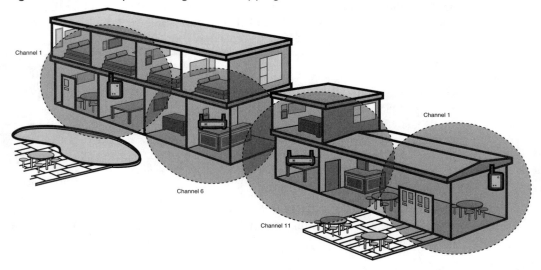

Keep in mind, when selecting the channels for your APs, that other wireless networks might be nearby. You also should plan your channel assignments based on any existing Wi-Fi signals that are in or around your designated coverage area.

NOTE   NetStumbler is free software that you can download from http://www.netstumbler.com to identify the channel settings of nearby APs and wireless routers.

If you are implementing a hotspot that needs to support many users in a dense area, such as in a huge auditorium filled with students who are accessing the web from their laptops, the overlapping channel situation might cause some difficulties. This is because you likely need to designate many APs in the dense area to support all the users. Even though a single AP might be able to handle more than 200 users connected to it at once, the throughput (speed) that each user experiences would be extremely low. When designating more than three APs in a single space, even though it might be in a huge auditorium, the cells of the APs will probably overlap with other cells. It is a problem only when cells on the same channel overlap.

TIP When many APs are colocated or when it is necessary to decrease their coverage or their cell size, you can turn down their transmitter power. In addition, you might want to make sure you are not using a high-gain antenna.

RF Propagation

You should be familiar with two different antenna types:

- Omnidirectional antennas
- Directional antennas

Omnidirectional antennas propagate the Wi-Fi signals the same in all directions. Most manufacturers provide this antenna type on their APs, wireless routers, and client devices. Omnidirectional antennas do well in most facilities.

Figure A-7 shows a pair of omnidirectional antennas.

Figure A-7   Example of Omnidirectional Antennas

Wireless networking vendors usually sell high-gain omnidirectional antennas (see Figure A-8 for an example) for use with their products. This allows a larger Wi-Fi coverage area in all directions.

Figure A-8   Example of a High-Gain Omnidirectional Antenna

Directional antennas, however, focus the Wi-Fi signals and provide much greater wireless coverage in one direction than in others. Unlike omnidirectional antennas, most directional antennas are external, meaning you need to mount the antenna somewhere and connect the antenna cable to the AP or wireless router. Figure A-9 shows an example of a directional antenna, called a *patch antenna*. Figure A-10 depicts how this antenna type might propagate the Wi-Fi signals.

Figure A-9   Example of a Patch Antenna

Figure A-10   Coverage Area of a Patch Antenna

A directional antenna is useful when you want more horizontal than vertical coverage, such as when providing coverage for a long set of offices.

RF Interference and Attenuation

One of the biggest challenges when working with wireless networks is the RF interference and attenuation. It takes practice to develop the skills necessary to predict the coverage and performance of wireless networks to aid in a proper installation. Keep in mind that 802.11 wireless devices share the airwaves with other wireless technologies that might cause significant interference with your wireless network or hotspot. The most common of these devices are as follows:

- 2.4-GHz cordless phones
- Wireless speakers and headphones
- 2.4-GHz baby monitors
- Microwave ovens
- Bluetooth devices

Using these devices in or around your wireless coverage area will likely degrade the performance of your network, or hotspot. In some cases, you might not even be able to keep a connection with the wireless network such as when using a wireless client next to an operating microwave oven. You can take some simple steps to help prevent these issues. Try to use cordless phones and other wireless devices in other frequency bands, such as 900 MHz or 5 GHz. Try not to use microwave ovens around APs or wireless clients. You might also avoid RF interference from microwave ovens by avoiding channel 11, because the top one-third of a band is typically affected the worst. You can also refrain from installing APs close to microwave ovens.

Attenuation, as discussed in this book, means the loss of radio signal strength. *Free space loss* is a type of attenuation that is the natural loss of the radio signal when propagating through the air without obstructions. As Figure A-11 illustrates, the signal gets weaker and weaker when traveling away from the AP.

Figure A-11 Depiction of Free Space Loss

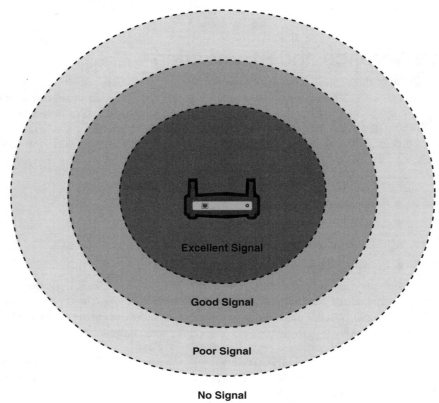

Excellent Signal

Good Signal

Poor Signal

No Signal

If buildings did not have walls, desks, filing cabinets, or elevators, it would be much easier to install wireless networks. This is because pretty much all you would have to think about would be free space loss when determining how many APs a facility needs, where to put them, and what antennas to use. However, this is not the case; buildings are usually filled with things that cause significant attenuation to your Wi-Fi signals. For instance, Figure A-12 shows how a wall might block RF signals.

Figure A-12 Attenuation from an Obstruction

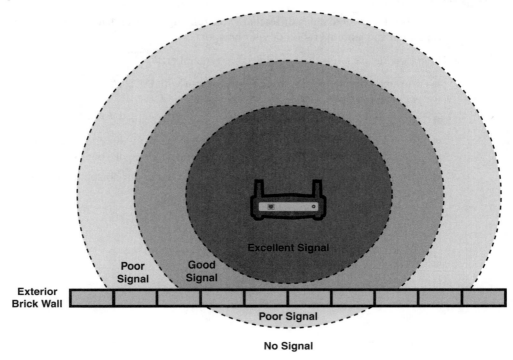

Suppose that you need good coverage on the other side of the brick wall, as shown in Figure A-12. You could replace the standard antennas on the AP with high-gain antennas. Then you would likely increase the signal quality enough to better penetrate the brick wall, and wireless clients on the other side would have a good connection. Alternatively, you could move the AP closer to the wall.

Final Review

This appendix covered many different factors relating to Wi-Fi that can help during the installation and administration of your hotspot.

The following are a few items you need to remember:

- Currently, implementing your Wi-Fi hotspot with 802.11g is your best bet until 802.11n has been completely standardized.

- Remember to use only the three nonoverlapping channels: 1, 6, and 11.

- Omnidirectional antennas propagate radio waves in all directions and are available in higher gains, which can increase the range of your hotspot.

- Other wireless devices can cause interference with your hotspot and other wireless networks.

Glossary

802.11 Written documents or standards formed by members of the IEEE to help wireless LAN manufacturers develop interoperable wireless products.

802.11a A wireless networking standard used for Wi-Fi devices. This standard specifies the use of the 5-GHz frequency band and data rates up to 54 Mbps. It is not interoperable with any other wireless networking standard.

802.11b A wireless networking standard used for Wi-Fi devices. This standard specifies the use of the 2.4-GHz frequency band and data rates up to 11 Mbps. It is interoperable with 802.11g.

802.11g A wireless networking standard used for Wi-Fi devices. This standard specifies the use of the 2.4-GHz frequency band and data rates up to 54 Mbps. It is interoperable with 802.11b.

802.11n An evolving wireless networking standard used for Wi-Fi devices. This upcoming standard specifies the use of the 2.4-GHz frequency band and data rates up to 540 Mbps. Wireless networking vendors have already started selling products based on this technology; these products are called pre-n or 802.11 draft products.

access point A device that provides Wi-Fi-capable end-user devices, such as laptops and PDAs, with wireless connections to a LAN or Internet connection. This device, unlike a wireless router, does not have routing capabilities and is used primarily in larger wireless networks.

ADSL (Asymmetric Digital Subscriber Line) An Internet connection in which the bandwidth is mostly devoted to the downstream, giving much faster download speeds than upload speeds. This is found most often in homes and small businesses.

beacon Beacons are sent by wireless networking devices, such as wireless routers and access points, via the airwaves. They provide a means of identifying access points (APs) and wireless routers to wireless clients. They contain pertinent information about the wireless network to inform nearby wireless clients of the network and to synchronize the wireless clients that are already part of the network.

data rate The speed or rate at which data is being sent or received over a network. Keep in mind that even though vendors or standards might claim data rates up to a certain rate (such as 54 Mbps), the real data rate might be half that amount, and this is not clearly determined. For example, the data rate under the Windows XP Wireless Status window is not necessarily the true speed you are experiencing.

default gateway A term commonly used in networks for the gateway in a network that is used to access another network (such as the Internet). It is typically a wireless or wired router.

DHCP (Dynamic Host Configuration Protocol) A protocol that manages and automates the assignment of network IP addresses and that allows devices to connect to a network and be automatically assigned an IP address.

dynamic IP address An IP address that changes periodically.

FTP A protocol that is designed to transfer files over a network or the Internet, for such applications as website management or file serving.

IP address A unique numerical code that devices on a network (local or Internet) must have to access the network. For example, Internet service providers (ISPs) give you either a static or dynamic IP address. If your Internet connection uses a dynamic IP address, it changes periodically. Each time you connect to the Internet, your network requests an IP address from the ISP's DHCP server. A valid IP address must be assigned to your connection before the Internet access can work.

MAC address   A unique code assigned to most forms of networking hardware (such as wireless routers and network adapters) for personal identification and for use among the "brains" of the network. For example, wireless networks use the MAC addresses of devices to identify themselves and the station to send information to.

NIC (network interface card)   Hardware (such as an Ethernet or wireless network adapter) that is installed in a computing device that enables it to communicate on a network. Remember that every NIC has a unique MAC address, enabling the identification of the device on the network.

PDA (personal digital assistant)   A small handheld computer that provides many applications, such as a personal organizer, e-mail access, and web access.

POP3 (Post Office Protocol)   A protocol that retrieves e-mail from a remote server over an Internet or network connection. POP3 requires the use of an e-mail client program, such as Microsoft Outlook. Many ISPs provide POP3 accounts to users.

RADIUS server   An Authentication, Authorization, and Accounting (AAA) protocol for network access or IP mobility applications. Hotspot administrators can use RADIUS servers to handle their network's accounting and roaming features.

SDSL (symmetric digital subscriber line)   An Internet connection that can provide the same amount of bandwidth both upstream and downstream, thus allowing a much greater upload rate than ADSL. This is commonly found in small or medium-sized businesses.

SMTP (Simple Mail Transfer Protocol)   A protocol for sending e-mail messages between servers. Most e-mail systems that send mail over the Internet use SMTP to send messages from one server to another; the messages can then be retrieved with an e-mail client using either POP or IMAP.

SSID (Service Set Identifier)   A wireless network name that the network infrastructure and user devices on the network use to personally identify the network.

SSL (Secure Socket Layer)   A protocol that encrypts information sent and received during an SSL session (on a local network or via the Internet). The most common use of SSL is to secure payment information during online transactions.

static IP address   An IP address that is indefinitely assigned to a network or Internet device.

subnet mask   Determines the subnet that an IP address belongs to and partitions the networks into segments. If you are not sure what mask to use, keep in mind that the default subnet masks (such as 255.255.255.0) that are used in wireless networking devices should be fine to use.

T1   Dedicated Internet connections commonly found only in large businesses where guaranteed bandwidth, or speed, is required. T1 lines offer good, reliable performance, but they are expensive.

VLAN   Keeps traffic from an application separate from other traffic while it is traversing the same physical network.

VPN   Typically used to securely connect remote networks or to give people secure connections to a remote network. All the information that is passed through the VPN tunnel is encrypted and secured from end to end (end-user device to the remote network).

WEP (Wired Equivalent Privacy)　A protocol that is designed to provide a wireless local-area network (WLAN) with a level of security and privacy comparable to that of a wired LAN by encrypting the data that is transmitted.

Wi-Fi　A term developed by the Wi-Fi Alliance to describe WLAN products that are based on the IEEE 802.11 standards.

Wi-Fi hotspot　Wireless networks intended to give the public wireless Internet access.

wireless router　A device that provides Wi-Fi-capable end-user devices, such as laptops and PDAs, with wireless connections to a LAN or Internet connection. The routing functions of this device allow it to be hooked up to the Internet (containing only an IP address); it can assign many IP addresses to the end users.

WPA (Wi-Fi Protected Access)　A data encryption method created by the Wi-Fi Alliance for wireless LANs. It is similar to WEP but is more secure.

Index

Numerics

802.11 standards, 14
  802.11a standard, 221
  802.11n draft products, 222
  comparing, 221–222

A

access points
  adding to hotspot, 178
  configuring for ZoneCD advanced free
    access hotspot solution, 84–87
  network and power connection options,
    189–190
  preinstallation site survey, 179–184, 187
  purchasing, 192
**access restrictions, configuring on wireless
  routers, 57**
accessing
  preferred network list, 205
  shared folders, 212
  web-based configuration utility on wireless
    routers, 53
acquiring signage, 135–136
active scanning, 224
adding
  ad-hoc networks to preferred network list,
    207–208
  preferred network to preferred network list,
    207–208
  shared printers to computer, 215
**ad-hoc networks, adding to preferred
  network list, 208–209**
**advanced options (preferred network list),
  210**
advertising, 137
  attracting users to hotspot, 19–20
    signage, 135–136

  revenue, generating, 20–21
  selling, 25
  submitting hotspots to online directories,
    137–141
aircraft, onboard Wi-Fi access, 10
airports, Wi-Fi access, 9
antennas
  directional, 229
  high-gain, 171
    installing, 175
    purchasing, 174–175
  omnidirectional, 229
**AP isolation, configuring on wireless
  routers, 55**
APs, 223
  beacons, 223–224
  configuring, 194
  installing, 194
  radio cells, 227
attenuation, 231–233
attracting users to hotspot, 19–20
  signage, 135–136

B

**backup files, configuring on wireless
  routers, 61**
**bandwidth restrictions, denying hotspot
  access to freeloaders, 145–146**
bandwidth throttling, 73
beacons, 223–224
**blocked services, configuring on wireless
  routers, 58–59**
blocking freeloader user accounts, 148
Boingo Wireless hotspot network
  commission structure, 22
  Hot Spot in a Box, configuring, 107–110,
    114
  revenue, estimating, 23

boot process, ZoneCD advanced free access hotspot solution, 89–97

broadband Internet connections, 6

businesses providing Wi-Fi access, 8

C

channels, 226–228

cities providing Wi-Fi access, 11

Closed mode, ZoneCD advanced free access hotspot solution, 68–70, 98–102

commission structure, Boingo, 22

companies providing Wi-Fi access, 10

comparing 802.11 standards, 221–222

configuring, 55

APs, 194

free or paid access and private network hotspot solution features, 127

wireless routers

access restrictions, 57

AP isolation, 55

backup files, 61

blocked services, 58–59

DHCP user limit, 54

remote management, 59

VPN passthrough, 56

ZoneCD advanced free access hotspot solution

access points, 84–87

boot process, 89–97

Closed mode, 98–102

Open mode, 97–98

connecting to wireless networks via Wireless Zero Configuration tool, 202

connection issues, troubleshooting, 166, 168

connection sequence for wireless clients, 225

creating private networks, 26

customers. See freeloaders

D

Dansguardian, 72

data rates, 221

denying hotspot access to freeloaders

with open/closed times, 143–144

with bandwidth restrictions, 145–146

with usage limits, 143

DHCP (Dynamic Host Configuration Protocol), 87

user limit, configuring on wireless routers, 54–55

directional antennas, 229

displaying user session details, 147–149

D-Link Airspot Wireless G Hotspot Gateway, 117

E

emphasizing usage terms to users, 146

enabling

shared folders, 211–212

shared printers, 214–215

Wireless Zero Configuration tool, 199–201

network adapter, 197–198

Entertainment Center Extenders, 27

estimating

fees for independent fee-based hotspots, 24

operating costs of hotspot hosting, 29–31

revenue

from Boingo, 23

indirect, 21–22

Ethernet cable, purchasing, 193

expanding wireless coverage

with additional access points, 178, 192–194

network and power connection options, 189–190

preinstallation site survey, 179–184, 187

with high-gain antennas, 171, 174–175

with wireless repeaters, 175–177

F

fee-based hotspots, 6

fees for independent fee-based hotspots, estimating, 24

file sharing
    enabling, 211–212
    shared folders, accessing, 212
free access hotspot solution
    setting up, 51–52
    wireless router, configuring, 53
free or paid access and private network
    hotspot solution, 117
    features, configuring, 127
    free access options, 118
    installing, 127, 130
    paid access options, 119–120
    required devices, 120
        hotspot gateway setup, 122–124
        RADIUS server setup, 126
        ticket printer setup, 125
    setting up, 118
    verifying proper operation, 130
freeloaders
    denying access to hotspots
        with open/closed times, 143–144
        with bandwidth restrictions, 145–146
        with usage limits, 143
    user accounts, blocking, 148
frequent disconnections, troubleshooting,
    164–165

G-H

gateways, installing, 128
general troubleshooting resources, 168
generating revenue, 20–21

high-gain antennas, 171, 229
    installing, 175
    purchasing, 174–175
HomePlug-certified devices, 190
Hot Spot in a Box, configuring, 107–110, 114
hotels, wireless access, 8
hotspot gateways
    as hotspot solution component, 120
    configuring, 122, 124

hotspots
    intangible costs of hosting, 30
    owner responsibilities
        content filtering, 156–158
        enable VPN passthrough, 155
        inform users of risk, 151–153
        isolate clients, 155–156
        provide safety tips, 154
        secure user information, 158
    user responsibilities, securing user informa-
        tion, 158–160
hotspot solutions, free or paid access and
    private network, 117
    features, configuring, 127
    free access options, 118
    installing, 127, 130
    paid access options, 119–120
    required devices, 120–126
    setting up, 118
household appliances, RF interference, 231

I

independent hotspots, 6
    fee-based, pricing, 24
indirect revenue, estimating, 21–22
installing
    APs, 194
    free or paid access and private network
        hotspot solution, 127, 130
    high-gain antennas, 175
    wireless routers
        as Boingo Wireless Hot Spot, 114
    ZoneCD
        preinstallation procedures, 76–83
        advanced free access hotspot solution, 88
intangible costs of hotspot hosting, 30
integrated mapping feature (online
    directories), 139
interference, troubleshooting, 164
intermittent disconnections,
    troubleshooting, 164–165

J-K-L

JiWire, 141

Linksys Wireless-G Broadband Router, 52
LiveCD, 65
locating hotspots
  online directories, 12
  Wi-Fi finders, 13–14
locations of typical hotspots, 7

M

MAC layer operation
  beacons, 223–224
  connection sequence, 225
  traffic reception and broadcasting, 225
  wireless client scannning, 224–225
media adapters, 27
mesh networking, 10
metropolitan Wi-Fi networks, 12
MIMO (Multiple Input Multiple
  Output), 222
monitoring Wi-Fi hotspots, 147
municipal networks, 10

N

NetStumbler, 228
network adapter
  connection status, checking
    via status window, 204–205
    via system tray, 203
  enabling/disabling
    via Start menu, 197–198
    via system tray, 198
nonoverlapping channels, 226–228

O

omnidirectional antennas, 229
online directories
  integrated mapping feature, 139
  JiWire, 141
  locating hotspots, 12
  submitting hotspot, 137–141
Open mode, 67–68
  ZoneCD advanced free access hotspot
    solution, 97–98
open/closed times, denying hotspot access to
  freeloaders, 143–144
operating costs, estimating, 29–31
operating systems, updating
  Windows XP, 197

P

passive scanning, 225
peer-to-peer networks. adding to preferred
  network list, 208–209
performance issues, troubleshooting,
  165–166
placement of gateway installation,
  selecting, 128
PoE (power over Ethernet), 193–194
poor performance, troubleshooting, 165–166
power line devices, purchasing, 192
preferred network list
  accessing, 205
  advanced options, 210
  preferred network, adding, 207–208
  preferred order, changing, 206
preinstallation procedures
  for ZoneCD installation, 76–83
  site surveys, conducting, 179–184, 187
presentation players, 28
preventing RF interference from
  household appliances, 231
printers, sharing, 214–215

private networks, creating, 26
probe requests, 224
PSPF (Publicly Secure Packet Forwarding), 55
Public IP discussion forum, 103–104
purchasing
  APs, 192
  Ethernet cable, 193
  high-gain antennas, 174–175
  PoE, 193–194
  power line devices, 192
  wireless repeaters, 177

R

radio cells, 227
RADIUS servers
  as hotspot solution component, 122
  configuring, 126
remote management, configuring on wireless routers, 59
reordering preferred network list, 206
responsibilities of hotspot owner
  content filtering, 156–158
  enable VPN passthrough, 155
  inform users of risk, 151–153
  isolate clients, 155–156
  provide safety tips, 154
  secure user information, 158
responsibilities of hotspot user, 158–160
restoring active hotspot in network list, 164
revenue
  Boingo commission structure, 22
  estimating, 21–22
  generating, 20–21
    via selling advertisements, 25
RF interference, 231
RF propagation, 229
RF space, 226–228
RSS (Rich Site Summary) feed, 74

S

security, SSL encryption, 27
selling advertising, 25
services offered by Public IP, 70–76
  bandwidth throttling, 73
  user classes, 73
setting up
  Boingo Wireless Hot Spot in a Box, 107–110, 114
  free access hotspot solution, 51–52
    wireless router, configuring, 53
shared folders
  accessing, 212
  enabling, 211–212
shared printers, 214
  adding to computer, 215
sign advertisements, acquiring, 135–136
simple free access hotspot solution
  setting up, 51–52
  wireless router, configuring, 53
solid cable, 191
SSID (service set identifier), broadcasting, 223
SSL encryption, 27
Start menu (Windows XP), enabling/disabling network adapter, 197–198
starting/stopping Wireless Zero Configuration tool, 201
status window, network adapter connection status, checking, 204–205
stranded cable, 191
submitting hotspot to online directories, 137–141
system tray (Windows XP)
  checking network adapter connection status, 203
  enabling/disabling network adapter, 198

T

ticket printers
  as hotspot solution component, 121
  configuring, 125
ticket system (ZoneCD), 74
time as intangible cost of hotspot hosting, 30
traffic flow in wireless networks, 225
troubleshooting
  connection issues, 166–168
  interference, 164
  intermittent disconnections, 164–165
  poor performance, 165–166
  resources, 168
  unlisted hotspot in wireless network list,
    163–164
typical hotspot users, 7

U

unlisted hotspots in wireless network list,
  troubleshooting, 163–164
updating Windows XP, 197
usage limits, denying hotspot access to
  freeloaders, 143
usage terms, emphasizing to users, 146
user classes (ZoneCD), 73
user session details, viewing, 147–149

V

verifying free or paid access and private
  network hotspot solution configuration,
  130
verifying ZoneCD configuration, 102
video cameras, 28
viewing user session details, 147, 149
VPN passthrough, configuring on wireless
  routers, 56

W-X-Y

Wayport, 6
web-based configuration utility, accessing,
  53
web-based configuration utility access
  server, 60–61
Wi-Fi Alliance, 14
Wi-Fi finders, 13–14
Wi-Fi hot zones, 10
Windows XP
  updating, 197
  Wireless Zero Configuration tool
    enabling/disabling, 199–201
    network adapter, enabling/disabling,
     197–198
    starting/stopping, 201
    wireless networks, connecting to, 202
wireless client scanning, 224–225
Wireless Media Players, 27
wireless network configuration, 15
wireless repeaters, 175–176
  purchasing, 177
wireless routers, 16
  access restrictions, configuring, 57
  AP isolation, configuring, 55
  backup configuration, 61
  blocked services, configuring, 58–59
  DHCP user limit, 55
    configuring, 54–55
  remote management, configuring, 59
  VPN passthrough, configuring, 56
  web-based configuration utility, accessing,
    53
  web-based configuration utility access
    servers, 60–61
Wireless Zero Configuration tool
  enabling/disabling, 199–201
  starting/stopping, 201
  wireless networks, connecting to, 202

Z

ZoneCD
advanced free access hotspot solution,
  65–104
    access points, configuring, 84–87
    Closed mode configuration, 98–102
    configuring, 89–97
    Open mode configuration, 97–98
    physical installation, performing, 88
Closed mode, 68–70
Open mode, 67–68
preinstallation procedures, 76–83
Public IP discussion forum, 103–104
services offered, 70–76
    user classes, 73
ticket system, 74

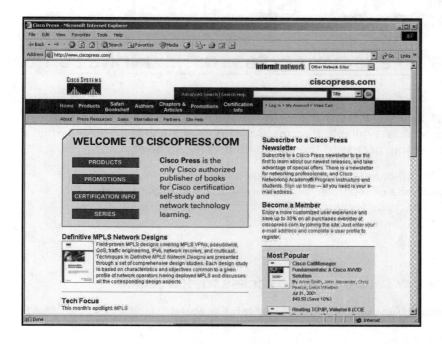

BOOKS ONLINE

ENABLED

THIS BOOK IS SAFARI ENABLED

INCLUDES FREE 45-DAY ACCESS TO THE ONLINE EDITION

The Safari® Enabled icon on the cover of your favorite technology book means the book is available through Safari Bookshelf. When you buy this book, you get free access to the online edition for 45 days.

Safari Bookshelf is an electronic reference library that lets you easily search thousands of technical books, find code samples, download chapters, and access technical information whenever and wherever you need it.

TO GAIN 45-DAY SAFARI ENABLED ACCESS TO THIS BOOK:

- Go to **http://www.ciscopress.com/safarienabled**

- Complete the brief registration form

- Enter the coupon code found in the front of this book before the "Contents at a Glance" page

If you have difficulty registering on Safari Bookshelf or accessing the online edition, please e-mail customer-service@safaribooksonline.com.